THE KEY

STUDENT STUDY GUIDE

athematics 6

THE KEY student study guide is designed to help students achieve success in school. The content in each study guide is 100% curriculum aligned and serves as an excellent source of material for review and practice. To create this book, teachers, curriculum specialists, and assessment experts have worked closely to develop the instructional pieces that explain each of the key concepts for the course. The practice questions and sample tests have detailed solutions that show problem-solving methods, highlight concepts that are likely to be tested, and point out potential sources of errors. **THE KEY** is a complete guide to be used by students throughout the school year for reviewing and understanding course content, and to prepare for assessments.

Copyright © 1999-2018 Castle Rock Research Corporation

Rao, Gautam, 1961 –
THE KEY – Mathematics 6 Alberta
ISBN: 978-1-77044-680-9

    1. Mathematics – Juvenile Literature. I. Title

Castle Rock Research Corporation
2000 First & Jasper
10065 Jasper Avenue
Edmonton, AB T5J 3B1

    10 9 8 7 6 5 4 3 2 1

Publisher
Gautam Rao

Contributors
Adam Boothe
Amanda Brouwer
Phyllis Kozak

Reviewers
Allison Finch

Dedicated to the memory of Dr. V. S. Rao

THE KEY – MATHEMATICS 6

THE KEY consists of the following sections:

KEY Tips for Being Successful at School gives examples of study and review strategies. It includes information about learning styles, study schedules, and note taking for test preparation.

Class Focus includes a unit on each area of the curriculum. Units are divided into sections, each focusing on one of the specific expectations, or main ideas, that students must learn about in that unit. Examples, definitions, and visuals help to explain each main idea. Practice questions on the main ideas are also included. At the end of each unit is a test on the important ideas covered. The practice questions and unit tests help students identify areas they know and those they need to study more. These questions can also be used as preparation for tests and quizzes. Most questions are of average difficulty, though some are easy and some are hard. Each unit is prefaced by a ***Table of Correlations***, which correlates questions in the unit (and in the practice tests at the end of the book) to the specific curriculum expectations. Answers and solutions are found at the end of each unit.

KEY Strategies for Success on Tests helps students get ready for tests. It shows students different types of questions they might see, word clues to look for when reading them, and hints for answering them.

Practice Tests includes three sample Provincial Achievement Tests divided into Parts A and B based on the entire course. These practice tests are similar to the format and level of difficulty that students may encounter on their Provincial Achievement Tests, allowing students the chance to practise for these tests. Answers and complete solutions are provided at the end of the section.

For the complete curriculum document (including specific expectations along with examples and sample problems), please visit *https://education.alberta.ca/mathematics-7-9/program-supports/*.

Castle Rock Research offers ***THE KEY Study Guide*** for many courses. Check our website www.castlerockresearch.com for a complete listing of books available for your area.

For information about any of our resources or services, please call Castle Rock Research at 1.800.840.6224 or visit our website at http://www.castlerockresearch.com.

At Castle Rock Research, we strive to produce an error-free resource. If you should find an error, please contact us so that future editions can be corrected.

CONTENTS

KEY Tips for Being Successful at School

KEY TIPS FOR BEING SUCCESSFUL AT SCHOOL

KEY FACTORS CONTRIBUTING TO SCHOOL SUCCESS

In addition to learning the content of your courses, there are some other things that you can do to help you do your best at school. You can try some of the following strategies:

- **Keep a positive attitude:** Always reflect on what you can already do and what you already know.

- **Be prepared to learn:** Have the necessary pencils, pens, notebooks, and other required materials for participating in class ready.

- **Complete all of your assignments:** Do your best to finish all of your assignments. Even if you know the material well, practice will reinforce your knowledge. If an assignment or question is difficult for you, work through it as far as you can so that your teacher can see exactly where you are having difficulty.

- **Set small goals for yourself when you are learning new material:** For example, when learning the parts of speech, do not try to learn everything in one night. Work on only one part or section each study session. When you have memorized one particular part of speech and understand it, move on to another one. Continue this process until you have memorized and learned all the parts of speech.

- **Review your classroom work regularly at home:** Review to make sure you understand the material you learned in class.

- **Ask your teacher for help:** Your teacher will help you if you do not understand something or if you are having a difficult time completing your assignments.

- **Get plenty of rest and exercise:** Concentrating in class is hard work. It is important to be well-rested and have time to relax and socialize with your friends. This helps you keep a positive attitude about your schoolwork.

- **Eat healthy meals:** A balanced diet keeps you healthy and gives you the energy you need for studying at school and at home.

How to Find Your Learning Style

Every student learns differently. The manner in which you learn best is called your learning style. By knowing your learning style, you can increase your success at school. Most students use a combination of learning styles. Do you know what type of learner you are? Read the following descriptions. Which of these common learning styles do you use most often?

- **Linguistic Learner:** You may learn best by saying, hearing, and seeing words. You are probably really good at memorizing things such as dates, places, names, and facts. You may need to write down the steps in a process, a formula, or the actions that lead up to a significant event, and then say them out loud.

- **Spatial Learner:** You may learn best by looking at and working with pictures. You are probably really good at puzzles, imagining things, and reading maps and charts. You may need to use strategies like mind mapping and webbing to organize your information and study notes.

- **Kinesthetic Learner:** You may learn best by touching, moving, and figuring things out using manipulatives. You are probably really good at physical activities and learning through movement. You may need to draw your finger over a diagram to remember it, tap out the steps needed to solve a problem, or feel yourself writing or typing a formula.

SCHEDULING STUDY TIME

You should review your class notes regularly to ensure that you have a clear understanding of all the new material you learned. Reviewing your lessons on a regular basis helps you to learn and remember ideas and concepts. It also reduces the quantity of material that you need to study prior to a test. Establishing a study schedule will help you to make the best use of your time.

Regardless of the type of study schedule you use, you may want to consider the following suggestions to maximize your study time and effort:

- Organize your work so that you begin with the most challenging material first.

- Divide the subject's content into small, manageable chunks.

- Alternate regularly between your different subjects and types of study activities in order to maintain your interest and motivation.

- Make a daily list with headings like "Must Do," "Should Do," and "Could Do."

- Begin each study session by quickly reviewing what you studied the day before.

- Maintain your usual routine of eating, sleeping, and exercising to help you concentrate better for extended periods of time.

CREATING STUDY NOTES

MIND-MAPPING OR WEBBING

Use the key words, ideas, or concepts from your reading or class notes to create a mind map or web (a diagram or visual representation of the given information). A mind map or web is sometimes referred to as a knowledge map. Use the following steps to create a mind map or web:

1. Write the key word, concept, theory, or formula in the centre of your page.

2. Write down related facts, ideas, events, and information, and link them to the central concept with lines.

3. Use coloured markers, underlining, or symbols to emphasize things such as relationships, timelines, and important information.

The following examples of a Frayer Model illustrate how this technique can be used to study vocabulary.

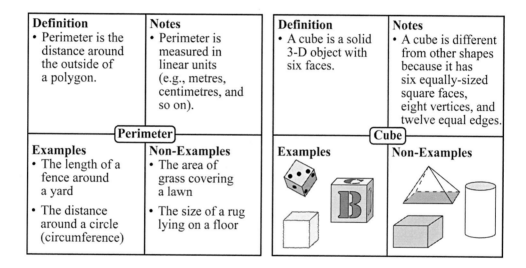

INDEX CARDS

To use index cards while studying, follow these steps:

1. Write a key word or question on one side of an index card.

2. On the reverse side, write the definition of the word, answer to the question, or any other important information that you want to remember.

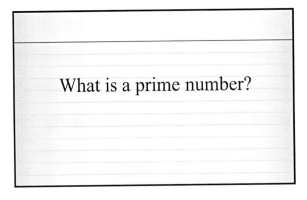

SYMBOLS AND STICKY NOTES—IDENTIFYING IMPORTANT INFORMATION

Use symbols to mark your class notes. The following are some examples:

- An exclamation mark (!) might be used to point out something that must be learned well because it is a very important idea.

- A question mark (?) may highlight something you are not certain about

- A diamond (◊) or asterisk (*) could highlight interesting information that you want to remember.

Sticky notes are useful in the following situations:

- Use sticky notes when you are not allowed to put marks in books.

- Use sticky notes to mark a page in a book that contains an important diagram, formula, explanation, or other information.

- Use sticky notes to mark important facts in research books.

MEMORIZATION TECHNIQUES

- **Association** relates new learning to something you already know. For example, to remember the spelling difference between dessert and desert, recall that the word *sand* has only one *s*. So, because there is sand in a desert, the word *desert* has only one *s*.

- **Mnemonic** devices are sentences that you create to remember a list or group of items. For example, the first letter of each word in the phrase "Every Good Boy Deserves Fudge" helps you to remember the names of the lines on the treble-clef staff (E, G, B, D, and F) in music.

- **Acronyms** are words that are formed from the first letters or parts of the words in a group. For example, RADAR is actually an acronym for Radio Detecting and Ranging, and MASH is an acronym for Mobile Army Surgical Hospital. HOMES helps you to remember the names of the five Great Lakes (Huron, Ontario, Michigan, Erie, and Superior).

- **Visualizing** requires you to use your mind's eye to "see" a chart, list, map, diagram, or sentence as it is in your textbook or notes, on the chalkboard or computer screen, or in a display.

- **Initialisms** are abbreviations that are formed from the first letters or parts of the words in a group. Unlike acronyms, an initialism cannot be pronounced as a word itself. For example, GCF is an initialism for **G**reatest **C**ommon **F**actor.

KEY STRATEGIES FOR REVIEWING

Reviewing textbook material, class notes, and handouts should be an ongoing activity. Spending time reviewing becomes more critical when you are preparing for a test. You may find some of the following review strategies useful when studying during your scheduled study time:

- Before reading a selection, preview it by noting the headings, charts, graphs, and chapter questions.

- Before reviewing a unit, note the headings, charts, graphs, and chapter questions.

- Highlight key concepts, vocabulary, definitions, and formulas.

- Skim the paragraph, and note the key words, phrases, and information.

- Carefully read over each step in a procedure.

- Draw a picture or diagram to help make the concept clearer.

KEY STRATEGIES FOR SUCCESS: A CHECKLIST

Reviewing is a huge part of doing well at school and preparing for tests. Here is a checklist for you to keep track of how many suggested strategies for success you are using. Read each question, and put a check mark (✓) in the correct column. Look at the questions where you have checked the "No" column. Think about how you might try using some of these strategies to help you do your best at school.

Key Strategies for Success	Yes	No
Do you attend school regularly?		
Do you know your personal learning style—how you learn best?		
Do you spend 15 to 30 minutes a day reviewing your notes?		
Do you study in a quiet place at home?		
Do you clearly mark the most important ideas in your study notes?		
Do you use sticky notes to mark texts and research books?		
Do you practise answering multiple-choice and written-response questions?		
Do you ask your teacher for help when you need it?		
Are you maintaining a healthy diet and sleep routine?		
Are you participating in regular physical activity?		

NUMBER

Table of Correlations				
Outcome	**Practice Questions**	**Unit Test Questions**	**Sample PAT Part A**	**Sample PAT Part B**
6N1.0 Develop number sense.				
6N1.1 Demonstrate an understanding of place value.	1	1, 2	*Part A of the PAT tests Number outcomes across grades 4, 5, and 6.*	28
6N1.2 Solve problems involving whole numbers and decimal numbers.	2, 3	3, 4, 5		29, 30
6N1.3 Demonstrate an understanding of factors and multiples.	4, 5	6, 7, 8		31
6N1.4 Relate improper fractions to mixed numbers and mixed numbers to improper fractions.	6, 7, 8	9, 10, 11		32, 33
6N1.5 Demonstrate an understanding of ratio, concretely, pictorially and symbolically.	9, 10	12, 13, 14		34, 35
6N1.6 Demonstrate an understanding of percent, concretely, pictorially and symbolically.	11, 12	15, 16, 17		36
6N1.7 Demonstrate an understanding of integers, concretely, pictorially and symbolically.	13, 14	18, 19, 20		37, 38
6N1.8 Demonstrate an understanding of multiplication and division of decimals.	15, 16, 17	21, 22, 23, 24	12, 13, 14, 15	39
6N1.9 Explain and apply the order of operations, excluding exponents, with and without technology.	18	25, 26		

6N1.1   Demonstrate an understanding of place value.

PLACE VALUE

The relationship between place values in any whole number or decimal number can be shown by a place value chart and base ten blocks or a place value chart and numerals.

When you move from right to left in the place value chart, the values increase by a factor of ten for each place value position moved.

Remember that each digit in a place value chart tells you something.

This place value chart shows the value of a digit (1) in each place value position.

Thousands			Ones		
Hundreds	Tens	Ones	Hundreds	Tens	Ones
100 000	10 000	1 000	100	10	1

× 10   × 10   × 10   × 10   × 10   × 10

Decimal numbers are parts of a whole number.

Ones	.	Parts of a Whole		
O	.	Tth	Hth	Thth
	.			
1	.	0.1	0.01	0.001

Always work from left to right when you are reading and writing numbers. Do not use the word *and* when you read or write whole numbers.

Example

Write sixty million sixty thousand sixty in numeric form.

Solution

Step 1

Determine the value of each part of the written number.

Sixty million is in the millions period. There are 6 ten millions in sixty million.

Millions			Thousands			Ones		
H	T	O	H	T	O	H	T	O
	6	0	0	0	0	0	0	0

Sixty thousand is in the thousands period. There are 6 ten thousands in sixty thousand.

Millions			Thousands			Ones		
H	T	O	H	T	O	H	T	O
				6	0	0	0	0

Sixty is in the ones period. There are 6 tens in sixty.

Millions			Thousands			Ones		
H	T	O	H	T	O	H	T	O
							6	0

Step 2

Put the periods together.

Add the sets of numbers to put the three periods together.

$$
\begin{array}{r}
60\ 000\ 000 \\
60\ 000 \\
+\quad\ \ 60 \\
\hline
60\ 060\ 060
\end{array}
$$

The numeric form of sixty million sixty thousand sixty is 60 060 060.

Read and write decimal numbers by naming the numbers and the place value position of the final digit.

The decimal point can be read as *decimal*, *point*, or *and*.

Example

Read and write in words the decimal number 1.257.

Solution

Step 1

Read the decimal number and name the place value of the final digit.

Follow these steps:

1. Say the word for the whole number: *one*.
2. Say the word *and* where the decimal point is.
3. Say the words for the three digits to the right of the decimal point: *two hundred fifty-seven*.
4. Say the word for the place value of the last digit: *thousandths*.

To read the decimal number 1.257, say one and two hundred fifty-seven thousandths.

Step 2

Write the decimal number in words.

Follow the same steps you used to read the decimal number. Instead of saying the words, write them down.

The decimal number 1.257 is written in words as *one and two hundred fifty-seven thousandths*.

---

1. The number 1 346 250 can be expressed in words as
   A. one million thirty-four thousand six hundred fifty

   B. thirteen million forty-six thousand two hundred fifty

   C. one million thirty-four thousand six hundred twenty-five

   D. one million three hundred forty-six thousand two hundred fifty

6N1.2   Solve problems involving whole numbers and decimal numbers.

PROBLEM SOLVING WITH WHOLE AND DECIMAL NUMBERS

When solving problems involving a whole number and a decimal number, the following strategies can be helpful:

- Simplifying the problem
- Looking for a pattern
- Drawing a picture
- Guessing, checking, and revising
- Making a table
- Using a calculator
- Working backward

Once you have decided on a strategy to use to help solve the problem, determine which operation the question is asking for.

Here are some terms to look for:

- The terms *product*, *multiply*, and *times* indicate a multiplication problem.
- The terms *quotient*, *divide*, and *divisible* indicate a division problem.
- The terms *sum* and *adding* indicate an addition problem.
- The terms *difference*, *less than*, and *more than* indicate a subtraction problem.

Here are some helpful hints for determining the operation:

- If given the total and asked for a part, know that division or subtraction is probably required.
- If asked for the total, know that multiplication or addition is probably required.
- If equal groupings are involved, know that multiplication or division is probably required.

Example

A movie store ordered 12 shipments of DVDs for the holiday season. There were 565 DVDs in each shipment.

Approximately how many DVDs were ordered in total? Explain the strategy used to obtain the estimation.

Solution

Step 1

Use the strategy of rounding each number to its greatest place value:

$12 \rightarrow 10$ because $2 < 5$, and $565 \rightarrow 600$ because $6 > 5$.

Step 2

Multiply the estimated number of shipments (10) by the estimated number in each shipment (600).

$10 \times 600 = 6\ 000$

About 6 000 DVDs were ordered.

Estimation is a good tool to use when problem solving to judge the reasonableness of an answer. Estimation is also a good tool to use when predicting a solution to a problem that does not require an exact answer.

Example

A case of pop costs $7.88. If a case contains 12 cans of pop, what is the estimated cost of one can of pop?

Solution

Step 1

Round the money amount to the nearest whole dollar.

$7.88 \rightarrow $8.00 because $8 > 5$.

Remember when you round money to the nearest dollar, you still include the decimal and two zeros because that is how money amounts are written.

Step 2

Round the number of cans of pop to the greatest place value, which is the tens place.
12 → 10 because 2 < 5.

Step 3

Identify the operation needed to solve the problem.

The total (the product) is given and needs to be divided into equal groups. The correct operation to use is division.

Step 4

Divide the estimated cost ($8.00) by the estimated number of cans (10).

A quick way to divide by 10 is to move the decimal one place to the left.
8.00 ÷ 10 = 0.80

The estimated cost of one can of pop is $0.80.

Use the following information to answer the next question.

> Mrs. Baker went to a computer shop with $2 000 to buy a computer and accessories. She finds a computer that costs $989 and a computer desk that costs $105. Before she makes the purchases, she estimates the amount of money that she will have left over.

2. Which of the following numbers is the **most reasonable** estimate of the amount of money Mrs. Baker will have left over?

    A. $800   **B.** $900

    C. $1 000   **D.** $1 100

Use the following information to answer the next question.

> Judy stacked 8 identical juice cans on top of one another. The height measured 177.6 cm.

3. To the nearest whole number, how tall is each juice can?

    A. 20 cm   **B.** 21 cm

    C. 22 cm   **D.** 23 cm

6N1.3   Demonstrate an understanding of factors and multiples.

MULTIPLES AND FACTORS

MULTIPLES

A **multiple** is the product of any given whole number and another whole number (except 0).
To determine the multiples of a given number, you can use multiplication, skip counting, or division.

For example, to find the multiples of 4, multiply 4 by 1, 4 by 2, 4 by 3, and so on. The multiplies are the products of these multiplication sentences.

A common multiple is the same multiple for two or more numbers. The **lowest common multiple** (LCM) is the smallest multiple that two numbers share.

Example

What is the lowest common multiple of 6 and 8?

Solution

Step 1

Determine the multiples of 6 and 8.

For 6, the multiples are 6, 12, 18, 24, 30, 36, 42, 48, …

For 8, the multiples are 8, 16, 24, 32, 40, 48, …

Step 2

Compare both lists of multiples to identify the numbers that are on both lists.

For 6: 6, 12, 18, 24, 30, 36, 42, 48

For 8: 8, 16, 24, 32, 40, 48

Two common multiples of 6 and 8 are 24 and 48.

Since 24 is the number that first appears on both lists, the least common multiple of 6 and 8 is 24.

FACTORS

A **factor** is a whole number that divides evenly into another whole number. Every number, except for 1 and 0, has the number 1 and itself as factors.

Common factors are factors that are the same for two or more numbers. The **greatest common factor** (GCF) is the largest factor that numbers share.

Example

What are the common factors of 27 and 30?

Solution

Step 1

Determine all the factors of 27.

$1 \times 27 = 27$

$3 \times 9 = 27$

The factors of 27 are 1, 3, 9, and 27.

Step 2

Determine all the factors of 30.

$1 \times 30 = 30$

$2 \times 15 = 30$

$3 \times 10 = 30$

$5 \times 6 = 30$

The factors of 30 are 1, 2, 3, 5, 6, 10, 15, and 30.

Step 3

Compare the two sets of factors to determine which factors appear on both lists.

Factors of 27: 1, 3, 9, 27

Factors of 30: 1, 2, 3, 5, 6, 10, 15, 30

The common factors are 1 and 3.

PRIME AND COMPOSITE NUMBERS

A **prime number** is any whole number whose only factors are 1 and itself.

A **composite number** is any whole number that has more than 1 and itself as factors.

The numbers 0 and 1 are neither prime nor composite.

Example

Use a hundreds chart to find how many prime numbers there are between 1 and 100.

Solution

On a hundreds chart, circle the prime numbers and shade the composite numbers.

Step 1

Cross out the number 1 because it is neither prime nor composite.

Step 2

Circle the number 2 because it is prime, and shade all the numbers divisible by 2 because they are composite.

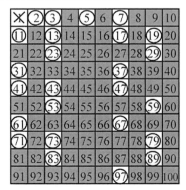

Step 3

Circle the number 3 because it is prime, and shade all the numbers divisible by 3 because they are also composite.

Continue circling the prime numbers and shading the numbers that are divisible by the prime numbers circled.

There are 25 prime numbers on the hundreds chart.

Prime factorization is the process of breaking down a product into its prime factors.

You can determine the prime factors of a composite number by using a **factor tree**. A composite number may have more than one form of factor tree.

Example
    Without using the factor of 1, complete a factor tree for 36.

Solution

Step 1
Think of all the whole numbers (except 1) that will equal 36 when multiplied by each other.
$2 \times 18 = 36$
$3 \times 12 = 36$
$4 \times 9 = 36$
$6 \times 6 = 36$

Step 2
Draw a factor tree for these combinations.

Remember to break all composite numbers into prime numbers.

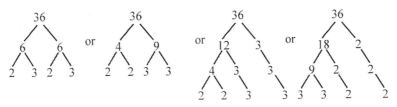

You can see that although the factors used are different (6×6, 4×9, 12×3, 18×2), the prime factorization is the same.
$3 \times 3 \times 2 \times 2$

---

4. Which of the following pairs of numbers are prime factors for both 45 and 60?
    A. 2 and 3   **B.** 2 and 5
    C. 3 and 3   **D.** 3 and 5

5. Which of the following numbers is **not** a common factor of 44 and 66?
    A. 1   **B.** 4
    C. 11   **D.** 22

6N1.4   Relate improper fractions to mixed numbers and mixed numbers to improper fractions.

IMPROPER FRACTIONS AND MIXED NUMBERS

A **proper fraction** is a fraction in which the numerator is less than the denominator.

An **improper fraction** is a fraction in which the numerator is greater than or equal to the denominator.

A **mixed number** consists of a whole number and a proper fraction.

Improper fractions and mixed numbers can be used to show the same amount.

Example

The given figure can be represented by a mixed number and an improper fraction.

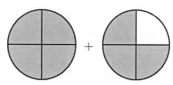

What improper fraction and mixed number can represent the shaded parts of the given fraction circles?

Solution

Step 1

Write the improper fraction that represents the shaded parts of the given fraction circles.
To determine the denominator, count the number of equal-sized parts in the fraction circles. There are 4 parts in each circle, so 4 is the denominator.
To determine the numerator, count the total number of shaded parts. There are 7 shaded parts in total, so 7 is the numerator.

The improper fraction that represents the shaded parts of the circles is $\frac{7}{4}$.

Step 2

Write the mixed number that represents the shaded parts of the given fraction circles.
To determine the whole number, count the number of circles that have all parts shaded. There is 1 whole circle shaded, so the whole number part of the mixed number is 1.
To determine the fraction, count the number of shaded parts out of the total number of parts in the second circle. There are 3 shaded parts out of 4 total parts. The fraction part of the mixed number is $\frac{3}{4}$.

The mixed number that represents the shaded parts of the circle is $1\frac{3}{4}$.

When converting a mixed number to an improper fraction, multiply the whole number by the denominator and then add the numerator. Put the total over the original denominator.

Example

Express the mixed number $4\frac{3}{5}$ as an improper fraction.

Solution

Step 1
Multiply the denominator (5) by the whole number (4).
$5 \times 4 = 20$

Step 2
Add the numerator to the product of the denominator and whole number.
$20 + 3 = 23$

Step 3
Write the improper fraction.

- The number 23 becomes the numerator of the improper fraction.
- The denominator of the improper fraction stays the same as the denominator of the mixed number (5).

$$4\frac{3}{5} = \frac{23}{5}$$

_____

When converting an improper fraction to a mixed number, divide the denominator into the numerator to find how many wholes you have. The remainder is how many parts you still have out of a whole.

Example

Write mixed numbers that represent the improper fractions $\frac{25}{6}$ and $\frac{11}{3}$.

Solution

Step 1
Determine the whole number.
Divide the numerator by the denominator.

For $\frac{25}{6}$, $25 \div 6 = 4$ R1.

For $\frac{11}{3}$, $11 \div 3 = 3$ R2.

Step 2

Determine the fraction.

Write the remainders as fractions $\left(\dfrac{\text{remainder}}{\text{divisor}}\right)$.

For $\dfrac{25}{6}$, R1 $\rightarrow \dfrac{1}{6}$

For $\dfrac{11}{3}$, R2 $\rightarrow \dfrac{2}{3}$.

Step 3

Write the mixed number.

Put the whole number and fraction together.

The mixed number $4\dfrac{1}{6}$ represents the improper fraction $\dfrac{25}{6}$.

The mixed number $3\dfrac{2}{3}$ represents the improper fraction $\dfrac{11}{3}$.

When comparing and ordering improper fractions and mixed numbers, it can be helpful to convert all the numbers into fractions with like denominators.

Example

Of the numbers $2\dfrac{1}{5}$, $\dfrac{8}{5}$, and $1\dfrac{2}{5}$, which has the **greatest** value?

Solution

Step 1

Change the two mixed numbers into improper fractions.

Multiply the whole number by the denominator of the fraction.

$2\dfrac{1}{5} \rightarrow 2 \times 5 = 10$

$1\dfrac{2}{5} \rightarrow 1 \times 5 = 5$

Add the numerator of the fraction to the product.

$2\dfrac{1}{5} \rightarrow 10 + 1 = 11$

$1\dfrac{2}{5} \rightarrow 5 + 2 = 7$

Write the result over the same denominator.

$2\dfrac{1}{5} = \dfrac{11}{5}$

$1\dfrac{2}{5} = \dfrac{7}{5}$

Step 2

Order the three improper fractions from smallest to largest.

Look at the numerators to determine the values.

$$\frac{7}{5}, \frac{8}{5}, \frac{11}{5}$$

The number with the greatest value is $\frac{11}{5} = 2\frac{1}{5}$.

---

6. Which of the following numbers has the **greatest** value?

   A. $\frac{18}{7}$ B. $\frac{14}{7}$

   C. $2\frac{5}{7}$ D. $1\frac{6}{7}$

7. Expressed as a mixed number, the improper fraction $\frac{55}{7}$ is

   A. $7\frac{1}{7}$ B. $7\frac{6}{7}$

   C. $8\frac{1}{7}$ D. $8\frac{6}{7}$

Use the following information to answer the next question.

Mrs. Ollie used $12\frac{2}{3}$ cups of flour to make some bread dough.

Numerical Response

8. When $12\frac{2}{3}$ is changed to an improper fraction, the numerator will be _____.

6N1.5   Demonstrate an understanding of ratio, concretely, pictorially and symbolically.

RATIOS

Ratios are used to compare two or more quantities. Ratios can be written using a colon (3:1), using the word *to* (3 to 1), or as a fraction $\left(\frac{3}{1}\right)$. The first number of the ratio is the first object in the comparison; the second number in the ratio is the second object in the comparison.

Example
   Write the ratio of unshaded circles to shaded circles in three different ways.

Solution

Step 1

Determine the order of the numbers.

Since the number of unshaded circles are mentioned first, the first number of the ratio will be 4.

Since the number of shaded circles is mentioned second, the second number of the ratio will be 5.

Step 2

Express the ratio in three different ways.

* 4:5

* 4 to 5

* $\frac{4}{5}$

A part-to-part ratio compares one part of the whole to another part of the whole.

Example
   Carlos draws a grid with some shapes in it.

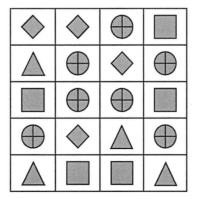

What is the ratio for circles to triangles?

Solution

Step 1

Count the number of circles in the diagram.

Since there are 7 circles, 7 will be the first number of the ratio.

7:?

Step 2

Count the number of triangles in the diagram.

Since there are 4 triangles, 4 will be the second number of the ratio.

7:4

The ratio of circles to triangles is 7:4.

A part-to-whole ratio compares one part of the whole to the whole.

Example

A Grade 6 class consists of 15 girls and 10 boys.

What is the ratio of girls to boys, and what is the ratio of boys to the whole class?

Solution

Step 1

Determine the part-to-part ratio of girls to boys.

The first number in the ratio represents the number of girls (15). The second number in the ratio represents the number of boys (10).

The part-to-part ratio of girls to boys is 15:10.

Step 2

Determine the part-to-whole ratio.

Determine the total number of students by adding the number of girls and boys in the class. This is equal to the whole.

15 + 10 = 25

There are 25 students in the class.

Write the ratio.

The first number in the ratio represents the number of boys (10). The second number in the ratio represents the total number of students in the class (25).

The part-to-whole ratio of boys to the number of students in the whole class is 10:25.

Ratios are usually reduced to lowest terms. You can do this by dividing both parts of the ratio by the same factor.

There are 80 students registered in Grade 6 at a particular school. Of those students, 50 are boys and 30 are girls.

9. The ratio of the total number of Grade 6 students registered to the number of boys in Grade 6 is

   A. 3:5   **B.** 3:8

   C. 5:8   **D.** 8:5

Use the following information to answer the next question.

Jennifer uses a diagram to represent all the cast and crew members for a school play.

Numerical Response

10. Write the ratio of crew members to cast members. _____

6N1.6   Demonstrate an understanding of percent, concretely, pictorially and symbolically.

PERCENTAGES

A **percentage** is a ratio that compares a quantity to 100. The symbol that is used to represent percent is %. For example, 50% means 50 out of 100 (50:100), where 50 is the part and 100 is the whole.

Example

Out of a group of one hundred students at Prairie School, 23% have blond hair, 12% have black hair, 54% have brown hair, and the rest have red hair.

What percentage of the students have red hair?

Solution

Step 1

Since a percentage is a ratio that compares a quantity to 100 and there are 100 students, add the percentages of students with blond, black, and brown hair.

$23 + 12 + 54 = 89\%$

Out of 100 students, 89% have blond, black, or brown hair.

Step 2

Since there are 100 students represented, the percentages need to add up to 100. Subtract 89% from 100% to determine the percentage of students with red hair.

$100 - 89 = 11$

Out of the 100 students, 11% have red hair.

Fractions, decimals, and percentages are all related. A percentage can be expressed as an equivalent ratio in fraction form or as an equivalent decimal number.

The following example shows how the same quantity can be represented by a percentage, a fraction, and a decimal.

This diagram is 40% shaded.

Since 40% represents 40 shaded parts out of 100 parts, the equivalent ratio in fraction form is $\frac{40}{100}$.

The fraction $\frac{40}{100}$ can be expressed as an equivalent decimal number: $0.40 \rightarrow 0.4$.

Example

Express 65% as a fraction and as a decimal.

Solution

Step 1

Express 65% as a fraction.

Since a percentage is a ratio out of 100, 65% can be explained as 65 parts out of 100 parts.

65:100

The ratio in fraction form is $\frac{65}{100}$.

$65\% = \frac{65}{100}$

Step 2

Express 65% as a decimal.

Since $65\% = \frac{65}{100}$ and $\frac{65}{100} = 0.65$, then $65\% = 0.65$.

All three can be explained as 65 parts out of 100 parts.

$65\% = \frac{65}{100} = 0.65$

Use the following information to answer the next question.

Four glasses are filled to various heights with chocolate milk.

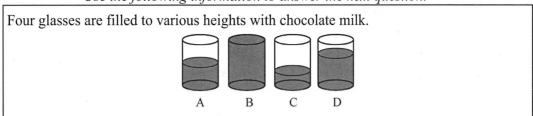

11. Which glass is about 50% filled with chocolate milk?

   A. A   **B.** B

   C. C   **D.** D

12. Which of the following fractions is equivalent to 64 %?

   A. $\dfrac{14}{25}$ **B.** $\dfrac{15}{25}$

   C. $\dfrac{16}{25}$ **D.** $\dfrac{17}{25}$

6N1.7   Demonstrate an understanding of integers, concretely, pictorially and symbolically.

INTEGERS

An **integer** is any positive whole number, the additive inverse of any whole number, and zero. A positive integer, which is represented by a positive sign (+), is any whole number and is greater than zero. A negative integer, which is represented by a negative sign (−), is the additive inverse of any whole number and is less than zero. Zero is neither positive nor negative; it is neutral.

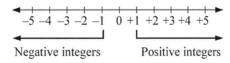

Example

   A set of integers:

   +4, −1, +2, −9

   From least value to greatest value, what is the order of the given integers?

Solution

Step 1

Separate the negative and positive integers.

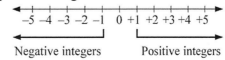

- The negative integers are −1 and −9.
- The positive integers are +2 and +4.

Step 2

Order the negative integers.

The negative integers that are farthest from the 0 have the least value. −9 has a lesser value than −1.

The order of the negative integers is −9, −1.

Step 3

Order the positive integers.

The positive integers that are farthest from the 0 have the greatest value. +4 has a greater value than +2.

The order of the positive integers is +2, +4.

Listed in order from least value to greatest value, the given integers are −9, −1, +2, +4

A number line is labelled with integers in increasing order from left to right. Positive integers are found to the right of zero. Negative integers are found to the left of zero. When comparing integers on a number line, the number farthest to the right is the largest. In order to determine the difference between two integers, begin with the digit in the ones place, and count ticks toward the other number.

Example

This number line is given.

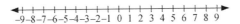

Draw an arrow above the given number line from −3 to the number that is 5 less than −3.

Solution

The value of a negative integer decreases the farther it is from 0.

Step 1

Start at −3, and count 5 ticks to the left.

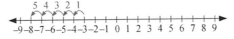

Step 2

Draw the arrow on the number line.

Start at −3, and draw a left-facing arrow (←) until you reach −8, which is 5 less than −3.

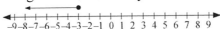

When comparing a set of integers, the symbol > is used to mean greater than, the symbol < is used to mean less than, and the symbol = is used to mean equal to.

Example

The following math statements are incomplete.

−3	_____	+3
	_____	−6
	_____	+4
	_____	+9

Complete the given statements using a < or > symbol.

Solution

Step 1

Negative integers are always less than positive integers.
−3 < +3
−8 < +9

Step 2

Positive integers are always greater than negative integers.
+4 > −1

Step 3

When comparing two negative integers, the closer a negative integer is to 0, the greater its value.
−6 > −7

___

One everyday example of using integers is measuring temperature on a thermometer.

Example

Order the numbers 15°C, –25°C, 0°C, and –5°C from coldest to warmest.

Solution

Step 1

Separate the positive and negative integers.

Positive temperatures: 15°C

Negative temperatures: –25°C, –5°C

Neutral temperatures: 0°C

Step 2

Order temperatures from coldest to warmest.

When dealing with temperatures, the farther the negative number is from 0, the colder the temperature. The farther away the positive number is from 0, the warmer the temperature. In order from coldest to warmest, the temperatures are –25°C, –5°C, 0°C, and 15°C.

13. Which of the following examples **cannot** be represented by the integer –5?

A. A loss of $5.00

B. A temperature of minus 5°

C. A road 5 km above sea level

D. A parkade 5 floors below ground level

14. Which of the following integers has the **lowest** value?

A. –4   B. –5

C. –6   D. –7

6N1.8   Demonstrate an understanding of multiplication and division of decimals.

MULTIPLYING AND DIVIDING DECIMAL NUMBERS

Estimation strategies are a useful tool when solving a multiplication or division problem. They can help you to determine whether your answer is reasonable.

ESTIMATING WITH DECIMAL NUMBERS

Some estimation strategies are rounding, rounding up, front-end estimation, and compatible numbers.

Rounding allows the numbers being estimated to be expressed to the nearest whole unit. To round up means to express the number being estimated to the next whole number.

Example

An art teacher bought 17.7 m of canvas for an art project. He cut the canvas into 6 equal lengths.

After the canvas was cut, about how long was each piece?

Solution

Step 1

Round the decimal number to the nearest whole number.

The decimal number 17.7 becomes 18 because 7 > 5.

Step 2

Estimate the answer.

The whole number 6 does not need to be rounded because 6 is a factor of 18.
$18 \div 6 = 3$

Each piece of canvas was about 3 m long.

Front-end estimation uses only the most significant (leftmost) digit of the numbers being estimated. All digits to the right are replaced by zeros.

Example

Use front-end estimation to divide 428 by 0.24.

Solution

Step 1

Use front-end estimation to round the numbers.

Keep the first value of each number, and change the remaining digits to 0.
428 → 400
0.24 → 0.20

Step 2

Remove the decimal from the divisor.

To remove the decimal from 0.20, move the decimal point one place to the right. After moving the decimal point one place to the right in the divisor, you must also move the decimal point in the dividend one place to the right.

$$0.20 \rightarrow 2.0 \qquad 400 \rightarrow 4000$$

Step 3

Divide the remaining numbers.
$4\ 000 \div 2 = 2\ 000$

The actual answer will be less than 2 000 since the values were rounded down.

The strategy of **compatible numbers** involves changing the numbers to be estimated to numbers that are close to the actual numbers, but easier to work with.

Example

Using the strategy of compatible numbers, estimate the product of 2.3 × 12.

Solution

Step 1

Determine compatible numbers for 2.3 and 12.

Since 2.3 is close to 2, let 2 represent 2.3.

Since 12 multiplies easily into 2, leave 12 as it is.

Step 2

Multiply the compatible numbers.

2 × 12 = 24

Using the strategy of compatible numbers, the product of 2.3 × 12 is about 24.

The actual product will be slightly higher.

OPERATIONS WITH DECIMAL NUMBERS

When multiplying decimal numbers, follow the same procedures you would use to multiply whole numbers.

To determine where the decimal point belongs, count the total number of digits to the right of the decimal point in your factors. The same number of digits should be to the right of the decimal point in your product.

Example

Emma has 8 straws. Each straw is 15.5 cm long. She decides to place the straws in a line on the table.

How long will the line of straws be if the straws are placed end to end?

Solution

Step 1

Multiply the length of one straw (15.5 cm) by the number of straws (8).

Write the numbers vertically.

Place the 8 below the 5 that is in the tenths place.

$$\begin{array}{r} 15.5 \\ \times\ 8 \\ \hline \end{array}$$

Step 2

Multiply 15.5 by 8, regrouping where necessary.

$$\begin{array}{r} {}^{4\,4} \\ 15.5 \\ \times\ \ 8 \\ \hline 1\ 240 \end{array}$$

Step 3

Place the decimal point in the solution.

Since there is one digit to the right of the decimal point in 15.5, you need to have one digit to the right of the decimal point in your answer.

1 240 → 124.0

$15.5 \times 8 = 124.0$

When the straws are placed end to end, the combined length of the 8 straws will be 124 cm.

To solve a division equation, remember to keep the decimal point in the quotient in line with the decimal point in the dividend.

Example

Whitney is throwing a surprise party for her grandmother's 80th birthday. Whitney plans to tie a ribbon onto each of 8 huge balloons, one for each decade of her grandmother's life.

If Whitney uses a roll of ribbon that is 9.6 m long and makes each ribbon for each balloon the same length, what will be the length of each ribbon? _____ m

Solution

Step 1

Write the expression that will solve the problem.

Divide the total length (9.6 m) by the number of equal-length ribbons needed (8).

$9.6 \div 8$

Step 2

Divide 9.6 by 8.

Be sure to line up the decimal points in both the dividend and the quotient.

```
      1.2
  8)9.6
   -8
   ──
    16
   -16
   ──
     0
```

Each piece of ribbon will be 1.2 m long.

---

15. Sharon and four of her friends are sharing the cost of a hotel room. The desk clerk informs Sharon that the total cost will be $197.52 to rent the room for one night. If the cost is divided evenly among them, what is the estimated amount that each person will need to pay?

    A. $20   B. $30

    C. $40   D. $50

Use the following information to answer the next question.

> Peter bought 9 pieces of string licorice. He measured them and found that each piece was 12.6 cm long.

16. The total length of string licorice that Peter bought was

    A. 108.4 cm   **B.** 108.9 cm

    C. 113.4 cm   **D.** 148.4 cm

Numerical Response

17. Use the strategy of compatible numbers to estimate the quotient of $106.2 \div 9$. _____

6N1.9   *Explain and apply the order of operations, excluding exponents, with and without technology.*

ORDER OF OPERATIONS

The standard order of operations is as follows:

1. Perform any calculations inside brackets (parentheses).
2. Perform any calculations involving multiplication and division, working from left to right.
3. Perform any calculations involving addition and subtraction, working from left to right.

Example

    Using the rules for order of operations, determine the value of the expression $4 \times 3 + 15 \div 5$.

Solution

Step 1

Complete the multiplication and division first, in the order they appear, from left to right.

It may be helpful to put brackets around the multiplication and division operations.
$(4 \times 3) + (15 \div 5)$

Perform the operations inside the two sets of brackets.
$(4 \times 3) + (15 \div 5)$
$= 12 + 3$

Step 2

Complete the addition and subtraction next, in the order they appear, from left to right.
$12 + 3$
$= 15$

---

18. The value of the expression $9 + 4 - 1 \times 9$ is

    A. 1   **B.** 2

    C. 3   **D.** 4

ANSWERS AND SOLUTIONS
NUMBER

1. D	6. C	11. A	16. C
2. B	7. B	12. C	17. 12
3. C	8. 38	13. C	18. D
4. D	9. D	14. D	
5. B	10. 13	15. C	

1. D

Step 1
Determine the ones period.
In the number 1 346 <u>250</u>, the digits 250 represent the ones period.
In words, 250 is written as two hundred fifty.

Step 2
Determine the thousands period.
In the number 1 <u>346</u> 250, the digits 346 represent the thousands period.
In words, 346 thousand is written as three hundred forty-six thousand.

Step 3
Determine the millions period.
In the number <u>1</u> 346 250, the digit 1 represents the millions period.
In words, it is written as one million.

Step 4
Starting with the millions period, put the three sets of written numbers together.
<u>one million three hundred forty-six thousand two hundred fifty</u>
In words, the number 1 346 250 can be expressed as one million three hundred forty-six thousand two hundred fifty.

2. B

Step 1
Round the costs of the computer ($989) and the desk ($105) to the greatest dollar value, or the greatest place value.
The number $989 is rounded up to $1 000, because 8 > 5.
The number $105 is rounded down to $100, because 0 < 5.

Step 2
Add the two estimated costs to determine the total estimated cost.
$1 000 + $100 = $1 100

Step 3
Subtract the total estimated cost from $2 000 to determine the estimated amount of money left after the purchases.
$2 000 − $1 100 = $900
The most reasonable estimate of the amount of money Mrs. Baker will have left over is $900.

3. C

Step 1
To determine the height of one can, divide the total height of the cans (177.6 cm) by the number of cans (8).
177.6 ÷ 8 = 22.2 cm

Step 2
Round the height of one can (22.2) to the nearest whole number.
22.2 → 22 because 2 < 5.
To the nearest whole number, the height of each can is 22 cm.

4. D

Step 1
You can use factor trees to help you break down the numbers 45 and 60 into their prime factors.

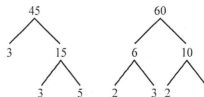

Step 2

Compare the two lists of prime factors.

Prime factors of 45: 3 and 5.

Prime factors of 60: 2, 3, and 5.

The numbers 3 and 5 are prime factors for both 45 and 60.

5. **B**

Step 1

First, you need to determine the factors of each number.

The factors of 44 are 1, 2, 4, 11, 22, and 44.

$1 \times 44 = 44$

$2 \times 22 = 44$

$4 \times 11 = 44$

The factors of 66 are 1, 2, 3, 6, 11, 22, 33, and 66.

$1 \times 66 = 66$

$2 \times 33 = 66$

$3 \times 22 = 66$

$6 \times 11 = 66$

Step 2

Compare the two lists of factors to see which of the given choices (1, 4, 11, 22) appear on both lists and which one does not appear on both lists.

The numbers 1, 11, and 22 are three of the four common factors (1, 2, 11, and 22) of the two numbers.

The number 4 is a factor of 44 but is not a factor of 66.

6. **C**

Before you can compare the numbers, you need to change them into the same type of number. Comparing improper fractions may be easier than comparing mixed numbers.

Step 1

To convert $2\dfrac{5}{7}$ into an improper fraction,

multiply the whole number (2) by the denominator (7) and add the numerator (5).

$(2 \times 7) + 5 = 19$

The denominator will stay the same.

$2\dfrac{5}{7} = \dfrac{19}{7}$

Step 2

To convert $1\dfrac{6}{7}$ into an improper fraction,

multiply the whole number (1) by the denominator (7) and add the numerator (6).

$(1 \times 7) + 6 = 13$

The denominator will stay the same.

$1\dfrac{6}{7} = \dfrac{13}{7}$

Step 3

Since the denominators are all the same, order the improper fractions by the numerators from least value to greatest value.

$\dfrac{13}{7}, \dfrac{14}{7}, \dfrac{18}{7}, \dfrac{19}{7}$

The number with the greatest value is $\dfrac{19}{7}$,

which is the mixed number $2\dfrac{5}{7}$.

7. **B**

To convert the improper fraction $\dfrac{55}{7}$ to a mixed

number, divide the numerator (55) by the denominator (7).

$55 \div 7 = 7 \text{ R}6$

The quotient (7) becomes the whole number of the mixed number.

The remainder 6 placed over the divisor (7) makes the fraction part of the mixed number.

$\dfrac{6}{7}$

Expressed as a mixed number, the improper

fraction $\dfrac{55}{7}$ is $7\dfrac{6}{7}$.

8. **38**

To change a mixed number to an improper fraction, multiply the whole number (12) by the denominator (3), and add the numerator (2).

$(12 \times 3) + 2 = 38$

The number 38 will be the numerator of the improper fraction. The denominator (3) will stay the same.

When $12\frac{2}{3}$ is changed to an improper fraction $\left(\frac{38}{3}\right)$, the numerator will be 38.

9. D

Step 1

For this ratio, you are comparing the whole to a part.
Whole:Part
Since you are comparing the total number of students (80) to the number that are boys (50), the total number of students will be the number to the left of the colon (:) and the number of boys will be to the right of the colon.
80:50

Step 2

A ratio is usually reduced to its lowest form. You can do this by dividing both parts of the ratio by the same number.
$80 \div 10 = 8$
$50 \div 10 = 5$
The ratio of the total number of students to the number of boys is 8:5.

10. 13

Step 1

Count the number of crew members.
Since there are 12 crew members, 12 will be the first number of the ratio.
12:?

Step 2

Count the number of cast members. Since there are 36 cast members, 36 will be the second number of the ratio.
12:36

Step 3

Reduce the ratio to its lowest terms. You can do this by dividing each side of the ratio by the same number, 12.
$\frac{12}{12}:\frac{36}{12} = 1:3$

The ratio of crew members to cast members is 1:3.

11. A

Glass A is half full, or about 50% filled with chocolate milk.

Glass B is full, or 100% filled with chocolate milk.

Glass C is less than half full, or about 25% filled with chocolate milk.

Glass D is more than half full, or about 75% filled with chocolate milk.

12. C

To change a percent to a fraction, put 64 over 100: $\frac{64}{100}$

You can see that the denominator in all the fractions is 25, so you must change $\frac{64}{100}$ to a fraction with denominator 25.

Since $100 \div 25$ is 4, you must divide both the numerator and denominator by 4:
$\frac{64 \div 4}{100 \div 4} = \frac{16}{25}$

The fraction that is equivalent to 64 % is $\frac{16}{25}$.

Therefore, alternative C is correct.

13. C

The integer -5 is a negative integer. Negative integers are used to represent things such as temperatures below the 0° mark on a thermometer, the spending of money, distances below sea level, and floors below ground level.

The example that cannot be represented by a negative integer is a road 5 km above sea level because it is a positive value.

14. D

The farther away a negative integer is from 0, the smaller the value of the integer will be.

The integer of -7 is farther away from 0 than -6, -5, or -4.

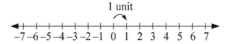

The integer that has the lowest value is -7.

15. C

To estimate the cost of the hotel, round $197.52 to $200, then divide by the total number of people paying.

$$\frac{200}{5} = 40$$

Each person would pay approximately $40.

16. C

To determine the total length of string licorice, multiply the length of one piece (12.6 m) by the number of pieces (9), regrouping where necessary.

$$
\begin{array}{r}
\scriptstyle 2\,5 \\
12.6 \\
\times\ 9 \\
\hline
113.4
\end{array}
$$

Since there is one digit to the right of the decimal in 12.6, there must also be one digit to the right of the decimal in the product 113.4.

Therefore, Peter bought 113.4 cm of string licorice in total.

17. 12

Step 1

Recall that compatible numbers are numbers that are close to the actual numbers and divide without a remainder.

A number that is compatible with 9 and is close to 106.2 is 108.

$(9 \times 12 = 108)$

Step 2

Divide the compatible numbers.

$108 \div 9 = 12$

The estimated quotient of $106.2 \div 9$ is 12.

Since the compatible number of 108 is a little greater than the actual number of 106.2, the estimated quotient will be a little less than 12.

18. D

Step 1

The Order of Operations tells you to perform the functions of multiplication and division first, in the order they appear, from left to right.

It may be helpful to first put brackets around the multiplication part of the expression.

$9 + 4 - (1 \times 9)$

$9 + 4 - (1 \times 9 = 9)$

$9 + 4 - 9$

Step 2

The Order of Operations tells you to perform the functions of addition and subtraction next, in the order they appear, from left to right.

$$9 + 4 = 13$$
$$13 - 9 = 4$$
$$9 + 4 - 1 \times 9 = 4$$

UNIT TEST — NUMBER

1. Represented as a decimal number, seven hundred seventy-nine thousandths is
   A. 0.700 79
   B. 0.0779
   C. 0.779
   D. 7.790

2. Represented in numeric form, the number three million four hundred five thousand six is
   A. 3 040 600
   B. 3 045 006
   C. 3 405 006
   D. 3 456 000

Use the following information to answer the next question.

> The daily attendance at a summer fair was 2 359 on Friday, 3 992 on Saturday, and 2 891 on Sunday.

3. Which estimate **best** represents the total attendance for the three days?
   A. 7 000
   B. 8 000
   C. 9 000
   D. 10 000

4. The approximate product of 136×56 is
   A. 1 500
   B. 1 600
   C. 5 000
   D. 6 000

Use the following information to answer the next question.

> Miss Bowen needs to buy 28 m of fabric to make new curtains for the windows in her house. The fabric costs $15.89 per metre.

5. Which of the following amounts is the **best** estimate for the cost of the fabric?
   A. $400.00
   B. $450.00
   C. $460.00
   D. $480.00

6. Which of the following numbers is a common factor of 18, 63, and 42?
   A. 2
   B. 3
   C. 6
   D. 7

7. Which of the following numbers is **not** a common multiple of 8, 12, and 16?
   A. 16
   B. 48
   C. 96
   D. 192

8. Which of the following expressions describes the prime factorization of 30?

   A. 5×6

   C. $2 \times 2 \times 3 \times 5$

   B. $2 \times 3 \times 5$

   D. $2 \times 2 \times 2 \times 5$

9. The improper fractions $\frac{7}{2}$ and $\frac{9}{4}$ can be respectively represented by the mixed numbers

   A. $3\frac{1}{2}$ and $2\frac{1}{2}$

   C. $3\frac{1}{3}$ and $2\frac{1}{4}$

   B. $3\frac{1}{2}$ and $2\frac{1}{4}$

   D. $5\frac{1}{2}$ and $5\frac{1}{4}$

10. Which of the following fractions has the **least** value?

   A. $\frac{73}{15}$

   C. $5\frac{3}{15}$

   B. $\frac{79}{15}$

   D. $4\frac{14}{15}$

Numerical Response

11. When the improper fraction $\frac{33}{4}$ is converted to a mixed number, the whole number

is _____.

Use the following information to answer the next question.

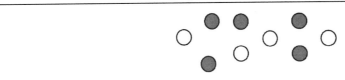

12. The ratio of the total number of circles to the number of shaded circles is

   A. 9:4

   C. 5:9

   B. 4:9

   D. 9:5

Use the following information to answer the next question.

John has 3 DVDs, 4 CDs, 7 books, and an orange in his bag.

13. What is the ratio of the number of DVDs to CDs in his bag?

   A. 1:2

   C. 3:2

   B. 1:3

   D. 3:4

Use the following information to answer the next question.

Shaylah uses black and grey markers to colour this grid.

14. Shaylah realizes that the ratio 5:4 can be used to describe the number of

    A. grey squares to the total number of squares

    B. grey squares to the number of black squares

    C. black squares to the number of grey squares

    D. black squares to the total number of squares

15. How is 52% expressed as a fraction?

    A. $\dfrac{2}{5}$ **B.** $\dfrac{1}{3}$

    C. $\dfrac{13}{25}$ **D.** $\dfrac{11}{21}$

16. What is the decimal equivalent of 8.2%?

    A. 820.0   **B.** 82.0

    C. 0.82   **D.** 0.082

Use the following information to answer the next question.

Strawberry ice cream is approximately 40% fat.

17. Write this percentage as a fraction in lowest terms.

    A. $\dfrac{40}{100}$ **B.** $\dfrac{20}{50}$

    C. $\dfrac{10}{25}$ **D.** $\dfrac{2}{5}$

Use the following information to answer the next question.

The given table shows the temperatures in four different towns in Alberta on a particular day in winter.

Town	Temperature (°C)
Camrose	5
Fox Creek	−5
Onoway	−1
Smoky Lake	0

18. In which town was the temperature a positive integer?

A. Onoway

B. Camrose

C. Fox Creek

D. Smoky Lake

Use the following information to answer the next question.

A set of integers is shown.
−10, −8, +9, −13

19. Which of the following number lines represents the correct order of the given integers?

A.

B.

C.

D.

20. In which of the following sets of integers do all four integers have a value less than −10?

A. −9, −8, −7, −6

B. −12, −9, −6, −3

C. −12, −11, −9, −8

D. −14, −13, −12, −11

Use the following information to answer the next question.

Marnie builds a tower out of 9 building blocks. Each block has a height of 7.6 cm.

21. How high is the tower that Marnie built?

A. 684 cm

B. 68.4 cm

C. 6.84 cm

D. 0.684 cm

22. What is the quotient of $92.4 \div 2$ using the strategy of front-end estimation?

A. 41

B. 43

C. 45

D. 48

Use the following information to answer the next question.

A relay team of 7 members ran a total of 132.3 m during their last practice run.

23. If each team member ran the same distance at the same speed, how far did each team member run?

    A. 1.89 m   **B.** 18.9 m

    C. 189 m   **D.** 0.189 m

Use the following information to answer the next question.

Kalen has 22.8 m of string. He plans to cut the string into 4 equal pieces to use for 4 different kites.

Written Response

24. How long will each piece of string be?

25. What is the value of the expression $8 \times 2 + 23 - 56 \div 7$?

    A. 27   **B.** 29

    C. 31   **D.** 33

26. The expression $20 \div 4 + 16 \times 2$ is equal to

    A. 36   **B.** 37

    C. 42   **D.** 44

ANSWERS AND SOLUTIONS — UNIT TEST

1. C	7. A	13. D	19. B	25. C
2. C	8. B	14. C	20. D	26. B
3. C	9. B	15. C	21. B	
4. D	10. A	16. D	22. C	
5. D	11. 8	17. D	23. B	
6. B	12. D	18. B	24. WR	

1. C

Step 1

Since there is no "and" in the written number, you know that there is no whole number. Therefore, the decimal number will start with 0 followed by a decimal point.

Step 2

Since the fraction part of the number ends with the word "thousandths," you know that there will be three digits to right of the decimal. 0._____

Step 3

The three digits that represent the words "seven hundred seventy-nine" are 779.

Putting the two parts together, "seven hundred seventy-nine thousandths" is represented by the decimal number 0.779.

2. C

Step 1

Start by determining the numeric form for each period (millions, thousands, ones).

- Three million is in the millions period. Its numeric form is 3 000 000.
- Four hundred five thousand is in the thousands period. Its numeric form is 405 000.
- Six is in the ones period. Its numeric form is 6.

Step 2

Add the three sets of numeric forms together to get the total numeric form.

```
   3 000 000
     405 000
 +         6
   3 405 006
```

The number three million four hundred five thousand six is represented in numeric form as 3 405 006.

3. C

Step 1

Since the alternatives are all numbers rounded to their greatest place values, round the numbers given in the problem to their greatest values.

- 2 359 → 2 000 because 3 < 5
- 3 992 → 4 000 because 9 > 5
- 2 891 → 3 000 because 8 > 5

Step 2

Add the three rounded attendances.

2 000 + 4 000 + 3 000 = 9 000

The total attendance for the three days is best represented by the estimate 9 000.

Step 3

To check the estimate, find the actual attendance and compare it to the estimate of 9 000.

2 359 + 3 992 + 2 891 = 9 242

The estimate of 9 000 is very close to the actual attendance of 9 242, showing that 9 000 was the best estimate.

4. D

Step 1

Round each factor to its greatest place value.

136 → 100 because 3 < 5

56 → 60 because 6 > 5.

Step 2

Multiply the two estimated numbers.

100 × 60 = 6 000

The approximate product of 136 × 56 is 6 000.

5. D

Step 1
Round the decimal number ($15.89) to the nearest whole dollar.
$15.89 → $16.00 because 8 > 5.
Round the whole number to the nearest ten.
28 → 30 because 8 > 5.

Step 2
Calculate the estimated total cost by multiplying the two estimated amounts.
$16.00 × 30 = $480.00

6. B

Step 1
Determine the factors of the number 18.
1 × 18 = 18
2 × 9 = 18
3 × 6 = 18
The factors of 18 are 1, 2, 3, 6, 9, and 18.

Step 2
Determine the factors of the number 63.
1 × 63 = 63
3 × 21 = 63
7 × 9 = 63
The factors of 63 are 1, 3, 7, 9, 21, and 63.

Step 3
Determine the factors of the number 42.
1 × 42 = 42
2 × 21 = 42
3 × 14 = 42
6 × 7 = 42
The factors of 42 are 1, 2, 3, 6, 7, 14, 21, and 42.

Step 4
Compare the three lists of factors to see which numbers appear on all three lists.

- The factors of 18 are 1, 2, 3, 6, 9, and 18.
- The factors of 63 are 1, 3, 7, 9, 21, and 63.
- The factors of 42 are 1, 2, 3, 6, 7, 14, 21, and 42.

The common factors of 18, 63, and 42 are 1 and 3. Only 3 is listed in all the alternatives, so the correct answer is 3.

7. A

Step 1
Determine the factors of all the alternatives.

- Factors of 16: 1, 2, 4, 8, 16
- Factors of 48: 1, 2, 3, 4, 6, 8, 12, 16, 24, 48
- Factors of 96: 1, 2, 3, 4, 6, 8, 12, 16, 24, 32, 48, 96
- Factors of 192: 1, 2, 3, 4, 6, 8, 12, 16, 24, 32, 48, 64, 96, 192

Step 2
Look to see which numbers are a multiple of 8, 12, and 16.
The number 16 has 8 and 16 as a factor, but not 12.
1 × 16 = 16
2 × 8 = 16
The numbers 48, 96, and 192 are all multiples of 8, 12, and 16.
8 × 6 = 48
12 × 4 = 48
16 × 3 = 48
8 × 12 = 96
16 × 6 = 96
8 × 24 = 192
12 × 16 = 192

8. B

Step 1
The number 30 is divisible by 2.
30 ÷ 2 = 15
This factorization can be shown by the following factor tree.

Since 2 is a prime number, it cannot be broken down any more, so that part of the factorization is complete.

Step 2

The number 15 is divisible by 3.

$15 \div 3 = 5$

The factor tree can be extended to show this part of the factorization.

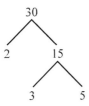

Since 3 and 5 are also prime numbers, the prime factorization is complete.

The expression $2 \times 3 \times 5$ describes the factorization of the number 30.

9. B

Step 1

Convert the improper fraction $\left(\dfrac{7}{2}\right)$ to a mixed number by dividing the numerator (7) by the denominator (2).

$7 \div 2 = 3.5 = 3\dfrac{1}{2}$

Step 2

Convert the improper fraction $\left(\dfrac{9}{4}\right)$ to a mixed number by dividing the numerator (9) by the denominator (4).

$9 \div 4 = 2.25 = 2\dfrac{1}{4}$

The improper fractions $\dfrac{7}{2}$ and $\dfrac{9}{4}$ can be respectively represented by the mixed numbers $3\dfrac{1}{2}$ and $2\dfrac{1}{4}$.

10. A

Before you can compare the fractions and mixed numbers, you need to change the two mixed numbers into improper fractions.

Step 1

To convert $5\dfrac{3}{15}$ into an improper fraction, multiply the whole number (5) by the denominator (15), and add the numerator (3).

$(5 \times 15) + 3 = 78$

The denominator will stay the same.

$5\dfrac{3}{15} = \dfrac{78}{15}$

Step 2

To convert $4\dfrac{14}{15}$ into an improper fraction, multiply the whole number (4) by the denominator (15), and add the numerator (14).

$(4 \times 15) + 14 = 74$

The denominator will stay the same.

$4\dfrac{14}{15} = \dfrac{74}{15}$

Step 3

Since the denominators are all the same, order the improper fractions by the numerators from least value to greatest value.

$\dfrac{73}{15}, \dfrac{74}{15}, \dfrac{78}{15}, \dfrac{79}{15}$

The fraction with the least value is $\dfrac{73}{15}$.

11. 8

Step 1

Divide the numerator by the denominator.

$33 \div 4 = 8 \text{ R1}$

Step 2

Determine the whole number.

When the numerator is divided by the denominator, the whole number quotient becomes the whole number of the mixed number.

Since the quotient is 8, the whole number of the mixed number is also 8.

$8 \text{ R1} \rightarrow 8\dfrac{1}{4}$

12. D

Step 1

Count the total number of circles.

There are 9 circles in total. 9 will be the first number of the ratio.

$(9:?)$

Step 2
Count the number of shaded circles.
There are 5 shaded circles. 5 will be the second number of the ratio.
(9:5)
The ratio of the total number of circles to the number of shaded circles is 9:5.

13. D

Step 1
Identify the units that are being compared.
The DVDs and CDs are being compared.

Step 2
Determine the order of the terms.
The number of DVDs is first, and the number of CDs is second.

Step 3
Write the ratio.
3:4

14. C

Step 1
Count the number of black squares, grey squares, and the total number of squares.
There are 20 black squares, 16 grey squares, and 36 squares in total.
Use these numbers to determine the ratios for each of the given choices. Remember that ratios are usually reduced to their lowest terms.
The given ratio of 5:4 is reduced to its lowest terms.

Step 2
Find the ratio for the comparison of black squares to grey squares.
Since there are 20 black squares and 16 grey squares, the ratio for the number of black squares to the number of grey squares is 20:16.
To reduce the ratio to its lowest terms, divide both numbers by 4 (the greatest common factor).
$20 \div 4 = 5$
$16 \div 4 = 4$
The ratio 5:4 can be used to describe the number of black squares to the number of grey squares.

15. C

Step 1
Write the value of the percentage over a denominator of 100.
The value of the percentage is 52, so it is the numerator.
$52\% = \dfrac{52}{100}$

Step 2
Reduce the fraction to lowest terms.
Divide the numerator and denominator by the greatest common factor (GCF). The GCF of 52 and 100 is 4.
$\dfrac{52}{100} = \dfrac{52 \div 4}{100 \div 4} = \dfrac{13}{25}$
Expressed as a fraction, 52% is $\dfrac{13}{25}$.

16. D

Step 1
Write the percentage as a fraction.
With a percentage, the denominator is always 100.
$8.2\% = \dfrac{8.2}{100}$

Step 2
Divide the numerator by the denominator (100).
$8.2 \div 100 = 0.082$
Therefore, the decimal equivalent is 0.082.

17. D

Step 1
Write the percentage as a fraction with a denominator of 100.
$\dfrac{40}{100}$

Step 2
Reduce the fraction to lowest terms.
Divide both the numerator and denominator by their greatest common factor.
$\dfrac{40 \div 20}{100 \div 20} = \dfrac{2}{5}$

18. B

On a number line, the positive integers are the whole numbers that are located to the right of 0. They may or may not be represented with a positive sign(+).

Although 0 is an integer, it is considered to be neutral, neither positive nor negative.

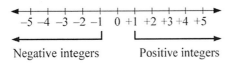

Recorded in the town of Camrose, the temperature of 5°C is a positive integer.

19. B

Positive numbers are represented to the right of 0. They get larger in value as they move away from 0. The integer +9 will be located 9 units to the right of 0.

Negative numbers are represented to the left of 0. They get smaller in value as they move away from 0.

The integers −13, −10, and −8 will be located 13, 10, and 8 units, respectively, to the left of 0.

This number line shows the correct placement of the given integers.

20. D

The farther the integer is to the left of the 0 on a horizontal number line, the smaller the value will be of the negative integer. This means that the integers that have a value less than −10 will all be located to the left of −10 on a horizontal number line.

The set of numbers in which all the integers have a value less than −10 is −14, −13, −12, and −11.

21. B

Step 1

To determine the height of the tower, multiply the height of one block by the number of blocks used to build the tower.

1 block = 7.6 cm
9 blocks = 7.6 cm × 9

Step 2

Calculate the product, regrouping where necessary.

Since there is one digit to the right of the decimal in 7.6, there must also be one digit to the right of the decimal in the product.

$$\begin{array}{r} 7.6 \\ \times\ 9 \\ \hline 68.4 \end{array}$$

The height of the tower is 68.4 cm.

22. C

Step 1

Use front-end estimation.

In front-end estimation, the first number (greatest place value) is kept and all numbers to the right are replaced with zeros. The decimal point and the numbers to the right of the decimal point are dropped.

$92.4 \rightarrow 90$

Step 2

Divide the estimated number by 2.

$90 \div 2 = 45$

Using the strategy of front-end estimation, the estimated quotient of $92.4 \div 2$ is 45.

23. B

Step 1

To determine the distance each member ran, divide the total distance by the number of runners.

7 runners = 132.3 m
  1 runner = 132.3 m ÷ 7

Step 2

Divide using long division.

When dividing, be sure to line up the decimal points in both the dividend and the quotient.

$$\begin{array}{r} 18.9 \\ 7\overline{)132.3} \\ \underline{-7} \\ 62 \\ \underline{-56} \\ 63 \\ \underline{-63} \\ 0 \end{array}$$

Each runner ran 18.9 m.

24. WR

To solve this problem, divide 22.8 by 4.

Divisor → $4\overline{)22.8}$ ← Quotient / Dividend

$$
\begin{array}{r}
5.7 \\
4\overline{)22.8} \\
\underline{20} \\
28 \\
\underline{28} \\
0
\end{array}
$$

Quotient ← 5.7
Dividend ← 22.8

Each piece of string will be 5.7 m long.

25. C

Step 1

According to the order of operations, do the multiplications and divisions first, in the order they appear, from left to right.

It may be helpful to put brackets around the multiplication and division parts of the expression.

$(8 \times 2) + 23 - (56 \div 7)$
$= 16 + 23 - 8$

Step 2

According to the order of operations, do the additions and subtractions next, in the order they appear, from left to right.

$16 + 23 - 8$
$= 39 - 8$
$= 31$
$8 \times 2 + 23 - 56 \div 7 = 31$

26. B

Step 1

According to the order of operations, do multiplications and divisions first, from left to right in the order in which they appear.

It may be helpful to put brackets around the division and multiplication parts of the expression first.

$(20 \div 4) + (16 \times 2)$
$= 5 + 32$

Step 2

According to the order of operations, do additions and subtractions next, from left to right in the order in which they appear.

$5 + 32 = 37$
$20 \div 4 + 16 \times 2 = 37$

NOTES

Patterns and Relations

PATTERNS AND RELATIONS

Table of Correlations

Outcome		Practice Questions	Unit Test Questions	Sample PAT Part A	Sample PAT Part B
6P1.0	Use patterns to describe the world and to solve problems.				
6P1.1	*Represent and describe patterns and relationships, using graphs and tables.*	1, 2	1, 2, 18	*Part A of the PAT tests*	1, 2
6P1.2	*Demonstrate an understanding of the relationships within tables of values to solve problems.*	3, 4, 5	3, 4, 5, 6	*Number outcomes*	3, 4
6P2.0	Represent algebraic expressions in multiple ways.			*across*	
6P2.3	*Represent generalizations arising from number relationships, using equations with letter variables.*	6, 7	7, 8, 9, 10	*grades 4, 5, and 6.*	5, 6
6P2.4	*Express a given problem as an equation in which a letter variable is used to represent an unknown number.*	8, 9, 10	11, 12, 13, 14		7, 8, 9
6P2.5	*Demonstrate and explain the meaning of preservation of equality, concretely and pictorially.*	11, 12	15, 16, 17a, 17b, 17c		10

6P1.1   Represent and describe patterns and relationships, using graphs and tables.

PATTERNS, TABLES OF VALUES, AND RELATIONSHIPS

A **pattern** is a repeated sequence of numbers, shapes, colours, or behaviours. Patterns can be represented visually with shapes, diagrams, or charts. When trying to represent or describe a pattern, it can be helpful to translate the pattern into a table of values. A completed **table of values** can be graphed to show the relationship between the **term** and the **term number**. The term is the value of a number in a pattern. The term number is the position of a term in a pattern.

Example

Jason makes a table of values by following this pattern rule. He starts with 7 and subtracts 2 from each term to get the next term.

Term Number	Term
1	7
2	
3	
4	

After completing Jason's table of values, plot the coordinates on the given graph.

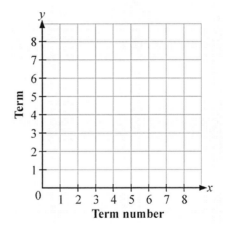

Solution

Step 1

Complete the table of values by applying the given pattern rule, which can be expressed as −2.

Term Number	Term
1	7
2	$7 - 2 = 5$
3	$5 - 2 = 3$
4	$3 - 2 = 1$

Step 2

List the ordered pairs. Remember that the term number is the first number in each ordered pair and the corresponding term is the second number in each ordered pair.
(1, 7)(2, 5)(3, 3)(4, 1)

Step 3

Plot the coordinates on the given graph.

- Start at 0, and move to the right along the *x*-axis until you reach the given term number.
- Move vertically until you reach the line that the given term from the *y*-axis is on.
- Make a dot where the two lines intersect.

This graph shows the coordinates plotted correctly.

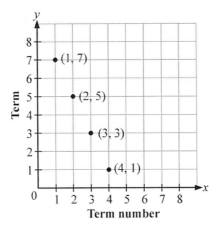

You can use tables of values and graphs to determine relationships among term numbers and terms. The main relationship usually described in a graph is the relationship between the term numbers and their corresponding terms. Such patterns are often more easily seen when presented in a graph.

Example

On the given graph, the minutes, as shown on the horizontal *x*-axis, represent the term numbers.

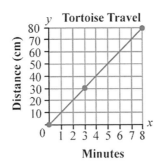

The distances the tortoise travels, as shown on the vertical *y*-axis, represent the terms.

What is the relationship between each term number and its corresponding term?

Solution

The relationship between each term number and its corresponding term is that each term number is multiplied by the constant, 10, to get its term value.

The number 10 is referred to as a constant because its value does not change.

The same operation by the same number ($\times 10$) is repeated for the whole pattern.

The relationship between the time and the distance is that for every minute, the tortoise travels 10 cm.

Use the following information to answer the next question.

A pattern is generated by starting with 3 and adding 2 to each term to get the next term.

Term Number	Term
1	3
2	5
3	7
4	9

1. If the *x*-coordinate is the term number and the *y*-coordinate is the corresponding term value, which of the following graphs correctly represents the pattern created by using the given pattern rule?

A.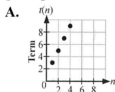

B.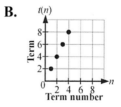

C.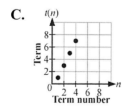

D.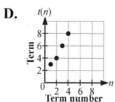

Use the following information to answer the next question.

The given graph shows the corresponding term numbers and term values of a pattern.

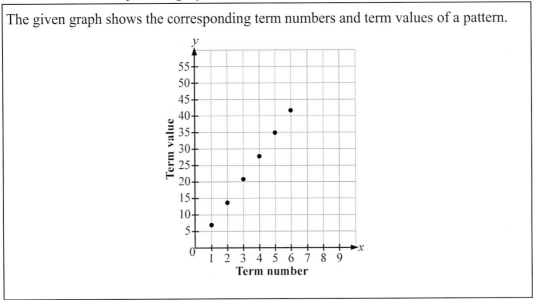

2. What is the term number with a term value of 35?

    A. 3   **B.** 4

    C. 5   **D.** 6

6P1.2   *Demonstrate an understanding of the relationships within tables of values to solve problems.*

USING A TABLE OF VALUES TO SOLVE PATTERN PROBLEMS

To determine a term for a given term number, you can extend the pattern in a table of values. A table of values is an organized way to show the term numbers (the sequence or order of the terms) and the terms (the numbers that make up the pattern).

Example

This diagram shows the first four figures of a pattern. The term number refers to the order of the figures. The terms refer to the total parts of each figure.

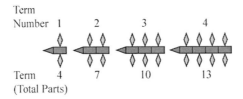

Create a table of values to help you predict the seventh term of the given pattern.

Solution

Step 1

Create the table of values.

Label the top row *term number*. Place the term numbers (1, 2, 3, 4) in the row.

Label the bottom row *term*. Place the corresponding terms (4, 7, 10, 13) in the row below the term numbers.

Term number	1	2	3	4
Term	4	7	10	13

Step 2

Determine the pattern rule.

A pattern rule describes how the numbers change from term to term. This pattern starts with 4, and 3 is added to each term to get the next term. The pattern rule can be described as term $+3$.

$4 + 3 = 7$
$7 + 3 = 10$
$10 + 3 = 13$

Step 3

Apply the pattern rule of term $+3$ for three more terms.

Term number	1	2	3	4	5	6	7
Term (total parts)	4	7	10	13	16	19	22

The seventh term of the pattern is 22.

Use the following information to answer the next question.

The given table shows the term numbers and corresponding term values of a pattern.

Term number	1st	2nd	5th	8th	9th
Term value	5	7	13	19	21

3. The term number with a term value of 15 is

    A. 3rd   **B.** 4th

    C. 6th   **D.** 7th

Use the following information to answer the next question.

The first five terms of a number pattern are shown in the given table of values.

Term Number	Term
1	92
2	85
3	78
4	71
5	64

4. If the pattern continues, what will the next term be?

    A. 60   **B.** 57

    C. 50   **D.** 47

Use the following information to answer the next question.

The given table shows the corresponding term numbers and term values of a pattern.

Term number	1	2	3	4
Term value	1	7	13	19

Numerical Response

5. What term number will have a value of 55? _____

6P2.3   *Represent generalizations arising from number relationships, using equations with letter variables.*

NUMBER RELATIONSHIPS EXPRESSED AS EQUATIONS WITH LETTER VARIABLES

An **expression** is a mathematical statement that may use numbers, variables, or both. A **variable** is a symbol or letter that stands for an unknown number. Translating a pattern rule or the relationship in a table of values into a mathematical expression can also be done using variables.

$$\underset{\text{Variable}}{\underbrace{2n}} = \underset{\text{Expression}}{\underbrace{6 + 12}}$$

Expression

Example

6, 12, 18, 24, 30, 36

If the letter x represents any given number in the pattern, write an expression that can represent the pattern rule used in the given number pattern.

Solution

In order to determine the pattern rule used, examine the numbers to see how they change from term to term.

$6 + 6 = 12$
$12 + 6 = 18$
$18 + 6 = 24$

The pattern rule is to add 6 to each term to determine the next term.

If the letter x represents any number in the pattern, then the expression $x + 6$ will represent the pattern rule being used.

The **commutative property of addition** means that $a + b = b + a$. In other words, the order in which numbers are added does not change the sum of the numbers.

Example

If $11 + 53 = 64$ and $j + 11 = 64$, then what is the value of the variable j?

Explain your answer.

Solution

The commutative property of addition states that changing the order of the numerals in an equation will not change the result.

If $11 + 53 = 64$, then $53 + 11 = 64$.

In the equation $j + 11 = 64$, the value of the variable is 53.
$j = 53$

The **commutative property of multiplication** means that $a \times b = b \times a$. In other words, the order in which numbers are multiplied does not change the product of the numbers.

Example

Mr. Green wrote these two equations on the board:

$4 \times 12 = 48$

$12 \times m = 48$

What is the value of the variable *m*?

Solution

The commutative property of multiplication states that if the order of factors is changed, the product stays the same.

If $4 \times 12 = 48$, then $12 \times 4 = 48$.

In the equation $12 \times m = 48$, the value of the variable *m* is 4.

DEVELOPING THE PERIMETER FORMULA

Since a rectangle has four sides, you can calculate the perimeter of a rectangle by adding the lengths of the four sides.

P = side 1 + side 2 + side 3 + side 4

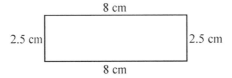

Since the opposite sides of a rectangle are the same length, you can determine the perimeter by multiplying the length by 2, multiplying the width by 2, and then adding the products.

perimeter = $(2 \times \text{length}) + (2 \times \text{width})$

You can also determine the perimeter by adding the length and width and then multiplying the sum by 2.

perimeter = $2(\text{length} + \text{width})$

You can now write formulas with letter variables for determining the perimeter of any rectangle.

- Let the variable P represent the perimeter of a rectangle.
- Let the variable l represent the length of a rectangle.
- Let the variable w represent the width of a rectangle.

Use one of these three formulas to solve for perimeter:

- $P = l + w + l + w$
- $P = (2 \times l) + (2 \times w)$
- $P = 2(l + w)$

DEVELOPING THE AREA FORMULA

Area is the number of square units needed to cover the surface of a rectangle, as shown in the diagram.

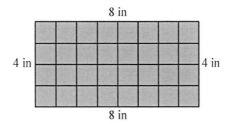

You can determine the area by counting the number of square units that cover the surface.

Another way to determine area is to count the number of square units in a row (the length of the rectangle) and multiply that number by the number of square units in a column (the width of the rectangle).

area= number of units in a row× number of units in a column

You can now write a formula with letter variables for determining the area of any rectangle.

- Let the variable A represent the area of the rectangle.
- Let the variable l represent the length of the rectangle.
- Let the variable w represent the width of the rectangle.

The formula for area is $A = l \times w$.

6. Which of the following expressions correctly represents the commutative property of addition?

   A. $3 + 7 = 2 \times 5 = 10$ **B.** $3 + 7 = 5 + 5 = 10$

   C. $3 + 7 = 7 + 3 = 10$ **D.** $3 + 7 = 13 - 3 = 10$

Use the following information to answer the next question.

The product of 24 and 9 is equal to the product of 9 and 24.

7. The given statement is an example of the
   A. associative law of addition   **B.** commutative law of addition

   C. associative law of multiplication   **D.** commutative law of multiplication

6P2.4 *Express a given problem as an equation in which a letter variable is used to represent an unknown number.*

VARIABLES

A **variable** is a symbol or letter that can be used to represent a unknown quantity or value in an equation. For example, in the equation $7 + k = 13$, the letter k is the variable. It represents the number that needs to be added to 7 to result in a sum of 13.

A **constant** is a value that does not change. For example, in the equation $5h + 3 = 13$, the number 3 is a constant. It will always have a value of 3 because it stands alone. The number 5 is not a constant because it is connected to a variable.

Example

An Equation

$a = b + c - 6$

How many variables and constants are there in the given equation? Explain your answer.

Solution

Step 1

Determine the variables.

Each of the three letters, a, b, and c, represent unknown quantities. Since each letter is different, each letter represents a different quantity, so there are three variables in the equation.

Step 2

Determine the constants.

Only the number 6 is a constant. It is referred to as a constant because it stands alone and its value will never change.

In the given equation, there are three variables and one constant.

A variable that represents an unknown quantity has only one possible value.

Example

Jane and Sue each have some cookies. Jane has four cookies, and together they have seven cookies. How many cookies does Sue have?

Express the problem as an equation using a variable, and then solve.

Solution

Step 1

Create an expression to represent the problem.

Jane has four cookies. Sue has some cookies. There are seven cookies in total. Let x represent the number of cookies Sue has.

$4 + x = 7$

Step 2

Solve for x.

$4 + x = 7$

$\quad x = 7 - 4$

$\quad x = 3$

Step 3

Determine if x could have another value.

The only value of x for which the equation $4 + x = 7$ is true is 3. Therefore, x must be equal to 3.

A variable that represents a changing quantity can have more than one value.

Example

Anna and Ned put all of their baseball cards together in a pile. There are four cards in the pile.

How many combinations of cards could Anna and Ned have?

Solution

Step 1

Create an equation to show the information.

Anna has ? baseball cards, and Ned has ? baseball cards. Together they have four baseball cards.

The equation $a + n = 4$ represents the known information.

The variable a represents the number of cards Anna has. The variable n represents the number of cards Ned has.

Step 2

Determine the possible values of a and n.

Think of all the whole numbers that can add up to 4.

$1 + 3 = 4$

$2 + 2 = 4$

$4 + 0 = 4$

Step 3

Determine all the possible combinations of cards.

There are five possible combinations of cards Anna and Ned could have.

Remember, a represents the number of cards Anna has and n represents the number of cards Ned has.

- a has a value of 1 when n has a value of 3.
- a has a value of 3 when n has a value of 1.
- a has a value of 2 when n has a value of 2
- a has a value of 4 when n has a value of 0.
- a has a value of 0 when n has a value of 4.

An **inverse operation** is an operation that has the opposite effect. Inverse operations undo each other, or cancel each another out.

For example, addition and subtraction are inverse operations. If $2 + 3 = 5$, then $5 - 3 = 2$.

You can use inverse operations to help you determine the value of a variable in an equation.

Example

Determine the value of the variable L in the equation $5 \times (L \div 2) = 30$.

Solution

Step 1

To determine the value of the variable, you need to get the variable by itself on one side of the equation. Since the variable is in brackets $(L \div 2)$, start by getting the bracketed expression by itself on one side of the equation. To do this, use the inverse operation of division $(\div 5)$ to cancel the value of 5. To preserve equality, perform the same operation $(\div 5)$ on the right side of the equation.

$5 \div 5 \times (L \div 2) = 30 \div 5$

$\qquad L \div 2 = 6$

Step 2

You can now get the variable by itself by using the inverse operation of multiplication $(\times 2)$ to cancel the value of 2. To preserve equality, perform the same operation $(\times 2)$ on the right side of the equation.

$L \div 2 \times 2 = 6 \times 2$

$\qquad L = 12$

Step 3

To check if equality has been preserved, replace the variable L with the number 12 in the given equation.

$5 \times (L \div 2) = 30$

$5 \times (12 \div 2) = 30$

$\qquad 5 \times 6 = 30$

$\qquad 30 = 30$

Since each side of the equal sign $(=)$ has the same value, equality has been preserved. The value of the variable L in the given equation is 12.

Use the following information to answer the next question.

Alexa has 88 math problems to solve. She can write 8 problems on each page of her notebook. She wants to know how many pages she will need to solve the 88 problems. She uses the letter k to represent the unknown in the equation.

8. In which of the following equations does the variable k **not** represent the unknown for the given problem?

A. $88 = k \times 8$

B. $8 \times k = 88$

C. $k \div 8 = 88$

D. $8 = 88 \div k$

Use the following information to answer the next question.

Jenny uses two balance scales to show the equality of objects in grams.

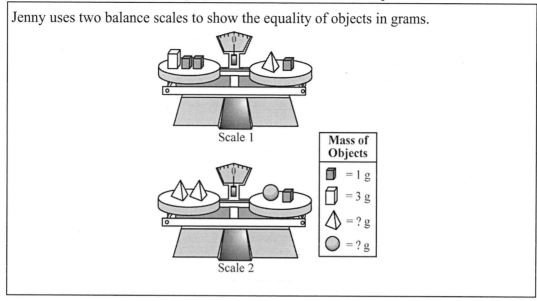

9. If the letter P represents the mass of the pyramid, then which of the following equations represents the equality shown on scale 2?

    A. $P = 3 + 1$ **B.** $2P = 7 + 1$

    C. $2P = 6 + 2$ **D.** $4P = 7 + 1$

Use the following information to answer the next question.

Each cube on the balance scale has a mass of 2 g.

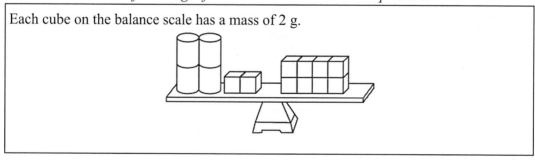

10. If the letter C represents the mass of one cylinder, then which of the following equations represents the equality shown on the given balance scale?

    A. $4C = 20$ **B.** $C + 4 = 20$

    C. $4C + 4 = 16$ **D.** $4 + C + 4 = 16$

6P2.5   *Demonstrate and explain the meaning of preservation of equality, concretely and*
           pictorially.

PRESERVING EQUALITY

In order to balance a scale and preserve equality, the objects on the left side of the scale must have a combined value equal to the combined value of the objects on the right side of the scale. In an equation, each side of the equal sign must balance. Remember that the equal sign really means "is the same as".

Example

   Scale A shows that four cylinders balance six blocks. Each cylinder weighs the same, and each block weighs the same.

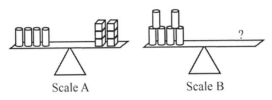

   Determine how many blocks are needed on Scale B to balance the six cylinders on the left side.

Solution

   Step 1

   Determine how many cylinders are equal to three blocks.

   Divide the number of cylinders and the number of blocks on the left side of Scale A in half. Dividing both sides in half will preserve equality.

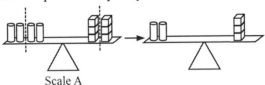

   The two cylinders will balance three blocks, as shown in the diagram. For every two cylinders, three blocks are needed.

Step 2

Determine how many blocks are equal to six cylinders.

Since there are three groups of two cylinders on the left side of Scale B and for every two cylinders three blocks are needed, nine blocks are needed on the right of Scale B to preserve equality.

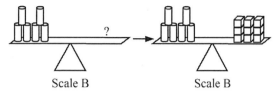

Scale B   Scale B

The right side of Scale B needs nine blocks to balance the six cylinders on the left side of the scale.

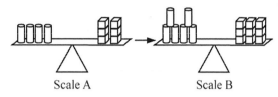

Scale A   Scale B

Use the following information to answer the next question.

In the given image, 3 hearts balance 2 triangles and 4 triangles balance 1 square.

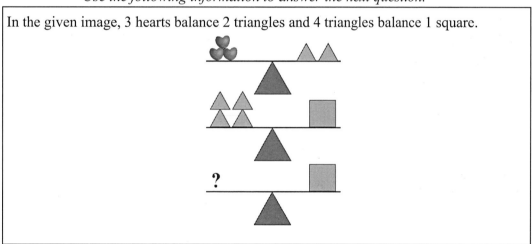

Numerical Response

11. How many hearts will balance 1 square? _____

Use the following information to answer the next question.

This balance scale is used to show equality.

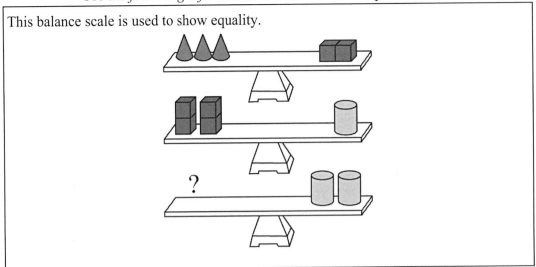

12. If 3 cones balance 2 cubes and 4 cubes balance 1 cylinder, then how many cones are needed to balance 2 cylinders?

   A. 8   B. 10

   C. 12   D. 14

ANSWERS AND SOLUTIONS
PATTERNS AND RELATIONS

1. A	4. B	7. D	10. C
2. C	5. 10	8. C	11. 6
3. C	6. C	9. B	12. C

1. A

Step 1

Complete the table of values by applying the pattern rule of adding 2 to each term to get the next term.

Term Number	Term
1	3
2	5
3	7
4	9

Step 2

Write the coordinates for the given pattern.

The first number in the ordered pair (to the left of the comma) will be the term number.

The second number in the ordered pair (to the right of the comma) will be the corresponding term.

(1, 3), (2, 5), (3, 7), (4, 9)

This graph shows the correctly plotted coordinates of the given pattern.

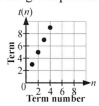

2. C

To determine the term number with a term value of 35, find the number 35 on the y-axis. Next, move horizontally toward the right until the point on the graph is reached. Now, move vertically down to the x-axis. The value found on the x-axis is the term number.

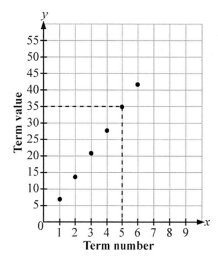

The term number with a term value of 35 is 5.

3. C

The given pattern is created by starting with 5 and adding 2 to each term to obtain the next term:

5, 7, 9, 11, 13, 15, 17, 19, 21…

The 6th term of the given pattern has a term value of 15.

4. B

Step 1

Determine the constant by which the terms in the pattern decrease.

To do this, determine the relationship between consecutive terms.

$92 - 85 = 7$
$85 - 78 = 7$
$78 - 71 = 7$
$71 - 64 = 7$

The pattern is generated by subtracting 7 from each term to get the next term.

The pattern rule can be expressed as -7, or term -7.

Step 2

Apply the pattern rule for one more term.
$64 - 7 = 57$

If the pattern continues, the next term will be 57.

5. 10

The given pattern is obtained by starting with 1 and adding 6 to each term to obtain the next term.

Continue the pattern rule of +6 until you reach the term that has a value of 55.

$19 + 6 = 25$
$25 + 6 = 31$
$31 + 6 = 37$
$37 + 6 = 43$
$43 + 6 = 49$
$49 + 6 = 55$

You have extended the given pattern shown in the table of values by six terms.
$4 + 6 = 10$

The 10th term of the given pattern has a term value of 55.

6. C

The commutative property of addition states that numbers can be added together in any order without changing the result.
$a + b = b + a$

There is only one case where just the order of the numbers being added is changed.

Therefore, the expression $3 + 7 = 7 + 3 = 10$ correctly represents the commutative property of addition.

7. D

The given statement is an example of the commutative law of multiplication. This means that $a \times b = b \times a$.

8. C

Step 1

First, determine how the unknown fits into the given problem.

You know the total number of problems that must be solved (88), and you know the number of problems that will be solved on each page (8). You do not know the number of pages that will be needed. This is the unknown that is represented by the letter k.

Step 2

Look at the equations that are given. When you solve each of these equations, the letter k represents the number of pages needed.

$88 = k \times 8$
$88 = 11 \times 8$
$8 \times k = 88$
$8 \times 11 = 88$
$8 = 88 \div k$
$8 = 88 \div 11$

When you solve the equation $k \div 8 = 88$, k does not represent the number of pages Alexa will need.

$k \div 8 = 88$
$704 \div 8 = 88$
$k = 704$

9. B

Step 1

Use the key to determine the equation that can represent the balance shown on scale 1.

The left side of the scale can be represented by the expression $3 + 1 + 1$.

The right side of the scale can be represented by the expression $P + 1$.

The balance shown on scale 1 can be represented by the equation $3 + 1 + 1 = P + 1$.

Step 2

Determine the value of P (the mass of the pyramid).

Subtract 1 from each side of the equation.

$3 + 1 + 1 - 1 = P + 1 - 1$

$3 + 1 = P$

$4 = P$

The mass of the pyramid is 4 g.

Step 3

Determine the equation that represents the balance shown on scale 2.

The left side of the scale can be represented by the expressions $2P$, $4 + 4$, or 8.

Since the right side of the scale must equal 8 and the cube has a mass of 1 g, then the sphere has a mass of 7 g.

$8 - 1 = 7$

The right side of the equation can be expressed as $7 + 1$ or 8.

Of the given options, the equation that represents the equality shown on scale 2 is $2P = 7 + 1$.

10. C

Step 1

Determine an expression that represents the left side of the balance scale.

If the letter C represents the mass of 1 cylinder on the left side of the scale, then $4C$ represents the mass of 4 cylinders on the left side of the scale.

Since each cube has a mass of 2 g, then the 2 cubes on the left side of the scale would have a combined mass of 4 g$(2 \text{ g} + 2 \text{ g} = 4 \text{ g})$.

Therefore, the left side of the scale can be represented by the expression $4C + 4$.

Step 2

Determine the mass on the right side.

There are 8 cubes on the right side of the scale, and each cube has a mass of 2 g.

$2 \times 8 = 16$

The eight cubes have a combined mass of 16 g.

Putting the two parts together, the equation that represents the equality shown on the given balance scale is $4C + 4 = 16$.

11. 6

Step 1

Determine the relationship between the hearts and triangles.

If 3 hearts = 2 triangles, then 4 triangles = 6 hearts. Twice as many triangles $(2 \times 2 = 4)$ equals twice as many hearts $(3 \times 2 = 6)$.

Step 2

Determine the relationship between the triangles and squares.

4 triangles = 1 square

Step 3

Determine the relationship between the hearts and squares.

If 4 triangles = 1 square and

4 triangles = 6 hearts, then

1 square = 6 hearts .

4 triangles = 6 hearts = 1 square

6 hearts are needed to balance 1 square.

12. C

Step 1

Determine the number of cones needed to balance 4 cubes.

Since 3 cones = 2 cubes, then

6 cones = 4 cubes.

The number of cones needs to be doubled because the number of squares is doubled.

2 cubes + 2 cubes = 4 cubes

3 cones + 3 cones = 6 cones

Six cones are needed to balance 4 cubes.

Step 2

Determine the number of cones needed to balance 1 cylinder.

Since 6 cones = 4 cubes and

4 cubes = 1 cylinder, then

6 cones = 1 cylinder.

Step 3

Determine the number of cones needed to balance 2 cylinders.

Since 6 cones = 1 cylinder, then

12 cones = 2 cylinders.

The number of cones needs to be doubled because the number of cylinders is doubled.

1 cylinder + 1 cylinder = 2 cylinders

      6 cones + 6 cones = 12 cones

To balance 2 cylinders, you would need to use 12 cones.

UNIT TEST — PATTERNS AND RELATIONS

Use the following information to answer the next question.

> **In** divided by 2 = **Out**

1. Which of the following tables follows the given rule?

A.
In	10	24	76	92
Out	5	12	39	47

B.
In	18	28	52	98
Out	9	14	26	48

C.
In	16	32	54	68
Out	8	16	27	35

D.
In	22	38	74	96
Out	11	19	37	48

Use the following information to answer the next question.

> The given graph shows the corresponding term numbers and term values for a particular pattern.
>
>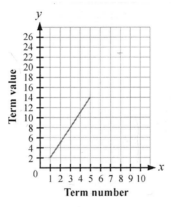

2. If the pattern continues, which term number will have a term value of 23?

A. 8   B. 9

C. 10   D. 11

Use the following information to answer the next question.

This table of values shows a pattern that starts with 5 with each term increasing by a particular constant.

Term Number	Term
1	5
2	15
3	45
4	135

3. What term number will have a value of 10 935?
   A. 7th
   B. 8th
   C. 9th
   D. 10th

Use the following information to answer the next question.

The given table lists the term numbers and values of a particular pattern.

Term number	1	2	3	4
Term value	5	9	13	17

4. If the pattern continues, which term number has a value of 29?
   A. 6
   B. 7
   C. 8
   D. 9

Use the following information to answer the next question.

A table of values is given.

Term Number	Term
1	3
2	6
3	12
4	?
5	?
6	?
7	?
8	?

5. The numeral 384 will be the
   A. 8th term
   B. 7th term
   C. 6th term
   D. 5th term

Use the following information to answer the next question.

| The pattern rule is to start with 4 and multiply each term by 3 to get the next term. |

Written Response

6. Using the given pattern rule, what term number will have a value of 972?

Use the following information to answer the next question.

$$7 \times 5 = x \times 7$$

7. For which value of x will the given equation be correct?
    A. 5   B. 6
    C. 7   D. 8

8. If Samantha is m years old now, which of the following expressions represents her age 8 years ago?
    A. $m - 8$ B. $m \times 8$
    C. $m + 8$ D. $m \div 8$

Use the following information to answer the next question.

| A number pattern is given. |
| 492, 495, 498, 501, 504, _____ |

9. If x is a number in the pattern, which of the following expressions can be used to find the next number?
    A. $x + 3$ B. $x + 4$
    C. $x \times 2$ D. $x - 3$

Use the following information to answer the next question.

> Jaymeson uses a pattern rule to create this number pattern.
> 23, 25, 22, 24, 21

10. Which of the following expressions describes the pattern rule that Jaymeson used?

    A. +3, −2   **B.** +2, −3

    C. +1, −3   **D.** +2, −4

Use the following information to answer the next question.

> Jen is thinking of a number. When she subtracts 10 from that number, there is a difference of 7. Mary wants to write an equation where the letter B represents the number Jen is thinking of.

11. Which of the following equations can Mary use to find out what number Jen is thinking of?

    A. $B - 10 = 7$ **B.** $B - 7 = 10$

    C. $B = 10 + 7$ **D.** $B + 7 = 10$

Use the following information to answer the next question.

> The sum of two numbers is 13 260. One of the numbers is 6 204, and the other number is unknown.

12. Which of the following equations **cannot** be used to solve the given problem?

    A. $13\ 260 - 6\ 204 = g$ **B.** $13\ 260 - g = 6\ 204$

    C. $6\ 204 + g = 13\ 260$ **D.** $6\ 204 + 13\ 260 = g$

Mikayla had 28 star stickers. She decided to give some of her stickers to her classmates. She chose a certain number of classmates and gave them each four stickers.
Mikayla used this array to determine how many classmates received stickers.

13. If k represents the number of classmates who received four stickers, then which of the following equations represents the strategy that Mikayla used to figure out how many classmates received stickers?

    A. $4 = k \div 28$ **B.** $28 = k \div 4$

    C. $k = 28 \div 4$ **D.** $k = 4 \div 28$

Use the following information to answer the next question.

Lora has three piles of dimes. She knows that there are 3 dimes in one pile and 25 dimes all together. She also knows that there are the same number of dimes in each of the other two piles. Lora writes the equation $d + d + 3 = 25$ to represent the number of dimes in the three piles.

Numerical Response

14. In the equation, the letter d is equal to _____.

Use the following information to answer the next question.

The given balance scale shows that the mass of two crackers is equal to the mass of six jellybeans.

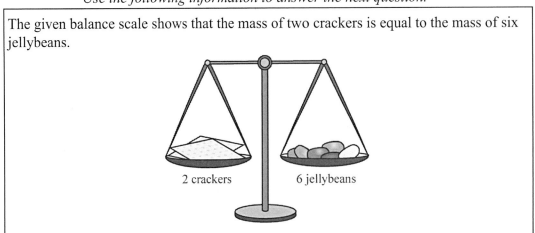

2 crackers   6 jellybeans

15. If the number of crackers is multiplied by 4, how many jellybeans would be needed to balance the scale?

A. 12   B. 18

C. 24   D. 28

Use the following information to answer the next question.

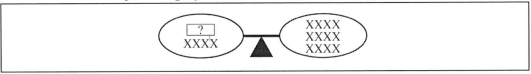

Written Response

16. If each **X** on the balance scale is equal to 2 g, then what is the mass of the rectangle?

Use the following information to answer the next multipart question.

17. At the circus, animals balance on a seesaw as shown in the diagram.

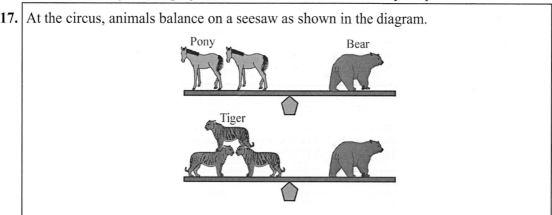

a) Which of the following statements about the information in the diagram is **false**?

   A. Two ponies are heavier than 3 tigers.

   B. Seven ponies are heavier than 3 bears.

   C. Three tigers weigh as much as 2 ponies.

   D. One bear weighs as much as 2 ponies or 3 tigers.

b) If 2 ponies balance 1 bear and 3 tigers balance 1 bear, then how many tigers will balance 6 ponies?

   A. 6   **B.** 9

   C. 10   **D.** 12

c) If 2 ponies and 2 bears are placed on the left side, how many tigers are needed on the right side to balance the seesaw?

   A. 9   **B.** 10

   C. 12   **D.** 15

Use the following information to answer the next question.

The given graph shows the term numbers and corresponding term values of a pattern that starts at 4 and continues by adding 6 to each term to get the next term.

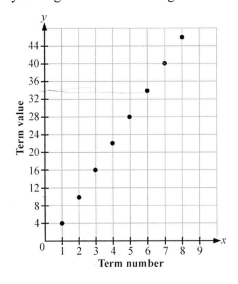

18. According to the graph, the term number with a term value of 34 is

   A. 4   **B.** 5

   C. 6   **D.** 7

ANSWERS AND SOLUTIONS — UNIT TEST

1. D	5. A	9. A	13. C	17. a) A
2. A	6. WR	10. B	14. 11	18. b) B
3. B	7. A	11. A	15. C	19. c) A
4. B	8. A	12. D	16. WR	20. C

1. D

To find the correct table, look at each **In** term and divide it by 2 to see if the **Out** terms match the pattern rule.

- In table, 76 ÷ 2 does not equal 39, so the table does not follow the pattern rule.
- In table, 98 ÷ 2 does not equal 48, so the table does not follow the pattern rule.
- In table, 68 ÷ 2 does not equal 35, so the table does not follow the pattern rule.
- In table, all of the In numbers divided by 2 equal the corresponding Out numbers, so the table follows the pattern rule.

2. A

The pattern can be continued by extending the line.

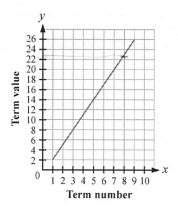

Term number

In this graph, the horizontal axis (*x*-axis) represents the term numbers, and the vertical axis (*y*-axis) represents the term values of the pattern.

Since the corresponding term number for the term value 23 needs to be found, draw a line parallel to the *x*-axis such that it cuts the *y*-axis at point 23.

From the point of intersection of this line and the line representing the pattern, draw a line parallel to the *y*-axis onto the *x*-axis. As shown in the graph, the vertical line cuts the *x*-axis at term number 8.

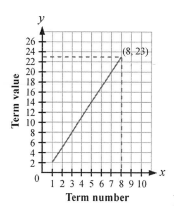

Term number

This implies that the corresponding term number for the term value 23 is 8; in other words, the 8th term of the given pattern has a term value of 23.

3. B

Step 1
Determine the constant by which the term values increase.
To do this, you need to determine the relationship between every two consecutive terms.
$5 \times 3 = 15$
$15 \times 3 = 45$
$45 \times 3 = 135$
The given pattern was generated by multiplying each term by 3 to get the next term. This rule can be expressed as ×3.

Step 2

Continue the pattern rule of ×3 to determine the next terms until you reach the term 10 935.

$$135 \times 3 = 405$$
$$405 \times 3 = 1\ 215$$
$$1\ 215 \times 3 = 3\ 645$$
$$3\ 645 \times 3 = 10\ 935$$

Step 3

Determine the term number that corresponds to the term value of 10 935.

The first four terms were given:

5, 15, 45, 135.

You determined the next four terms:

405, 1 215, 3 645, 10 935.

$$4 + 4 = 8$$

The 8th term has a value of 10 935.

4. **B**

The given pattern is made by starting at 5 and adding 4 to each term in order to obtain the next term of the pattern.

 1st term = 5
2nd term = 5 + 4 = 9
3rd term = 9 + 4 = 13
4th term = 13 + 4 = 17
5th term = 17 + 4 = 21
6th term = 21 + 4 = 25
7th term = 25 + 4 = 29

The value of the 7th term of the given pattern is 29.

5. **A**

Step 1

Before you can extend the pattern, you need to determine the pattern rule being used. Examine how the numbers change from term to term.

$$3 \times 2 = 6$$
$$6 \times 2 = 12$$

The pattern rule is multiply each term by *2* to get the next term.

Step 2

Continue the pattern rule to determine the 4th to 8th term numbers.

Term Number	Term
4	24
5	48
6	96
7	192
8	384

The numeral 384 will be the 8th term.

6. **WR**

Step 1

Make a table of values.

Start with 4 for the first term, and apply the pattern rule until you reach the term 972.

Term Number	Term
1	4
	12
	36
	108
	324
	972

Step 2

Continuing from 1, fill in the term numbers until you reach the term number that corresponds to the term 972.

Term Number	Term
1	4
2	12
3	36
4	108
5	324
6	972

The 6th term number will have a value of 972.

7. A

The given equation is illustrating the commutative property.

The commutative property of multiplication states that $a \times b = b \times a$.

The value of x must be 5 in order for the given equation to be true.

It will look like this: $7 \times 5 = 5 \times 7$.

8. A

Step 1

Determine the operation needed to write the equation.

Eight years ago, Samantha was eight years younger than she is today.

To determine her age eight years ago, subtract 8 from the age she is now.

Step 2

Write the equation that expresses Samantha's age eight years ago.

Since m represents Samantha's age today, the expression $m - 8$ represents her age eight years ago.

9. A

Step 1

Identify the pattern rule illustrated by the set of numbers.

The pattern starts with 492 and adds 3 to each term to get the next number.
$492 + 3 = 495$
$495 + 3 = 498$
$498 + 3 = 501$
$501 + 3 = 504$

Step 2

Identify the expression that can be used to determine the next number in the pattern.

The pattern adds 3 to each term in order to get the next number. If x represents the previous term, add 3 to x to get the next number in the pattern.

The expression used to find the next number is $x + 3$.

10. B

Step 1

Examine how the numbers change from one term to the next term so that you can determine the pattern rule used.
$23 + 2 = 25$
$25 - 3 = 22$
$22 + 2 = 24$
$24 - 3 = 21$

The pattern rule Jaymeson used was to add 2 to the first term (23) to get the second term (25) and to subtract 3 from the second term (25) to get the third term (22). She then repeated the process.

Step 2

The pattern rule has two parts.

The first part is to add 2. This can be expressed as +2.

The second part is to subtract 3. This can be expressed as −3.

The expression that describes the pattern rule is +2, −3.

11. A

Sort through the information to write a formula that can be used to find the number Jen is thinking of.

The number Jen is thinking of is represented by the letter B, which is the unknown number.

Subtracting 10 from the unknown number B is represented by the expression $B - 10$.

The difference of 7 is represented by $= 7$.

Mary can use the equation $B - 10 = 7$ to find the number Jen is thinking of.

12. D

Step 1

The letter g represents the unknown number that when added to 6 204 will result in the sum of 13 260.

These equations can be used to solve the given problem.
part + part = whole
$6\ 204 + g = 13\ 260$
$g + 6\ 204 = 13\ 260$

Step 2

Since subtraction is the inverse operation of addition, the letter g has the same value in these equations.

These equations can be used to solve the given problem.

whole − part = part

13 260 − g = 6 204

13 260 − 6 204 = g

The equation that cannot be used to solve the given problem is 6 204 + 13 260 = g.

You cannot add the whole to a part of the whole and get another part of the same whole.

13. **C**

In the equation, the unknown number of classmates who received stickers is represented by k.

There are 28 stars in Mikayla's array. If each chosen classmate got four stickers, then Mikayla will divide the 28 stickers into groups of four.

The equation that represents the strategy Mikayla used to determine how many students received stickers is $k = 28 \div 4$.

14. **11**

Step 1

Isolate the variables.

To isolate the variables on the left side of the equation, subtract 3 from both sides of the equation.

$d + d + 3 - 3 = 25 - 3$

$d + d = 22$

Step 2

Determine the value of d.

Since there are two variables that have the same value, divide 22 by 2 to determine the value of each variable.

$22 \div 2 = 11$

The value of d is equal to 11.

Step 3

Check your work.

Substitute the number 11 into the equation Lora wrote.

$d + d + 3 = 25$

$11 + 11 + 3 = 25$

$25 = 25$

Two of the piles had 11 dimes each.

15. **C**

Step 1

Identify the relationship between the number of crackers and the number of jellybeans.

An equation that can represent this relationship is 2 crackers = 6 jellybeans.

Step 2

Determine what will happen to the number of jellybeans if the number of crackers is multiplied by 4.

To preserve the equality of the equation, you need to perform the same operation to both sides of the equation. Since you are increasing the number of crackers by multiplying by 4, you also need to multiply the number of jellybeans by 4.

2 crackers × 4 = 6 jellybeans × 4

8 crackers = 24 jellybeans

If the number of crackers is multiplied by 4, then 24 jellybeans will balance the scale.

16. **WR**

Step 1

Use the inverse operation of subtraction and remove four Xs from each side of the scale. This will preserve equality.

The left side of the scale will now have only the variable (the rectangle).

$4 - 4 = 0$

The right side of the scale will now have eight Xs.

$12 - 4 = 8$

The rectangle on the left side of the scale is equal in value to the eight Xs on the right side of the scale.

Step 2

Since each X is equal to 2 g, count by 2s for each of the eight Xs.

2, 4, 6, 8, 10, 12, 14, 16

The mass of the rectangle is 16 g.

Step 3

You can check that equality has been preserved by replacing the rectangle (in the original equation) with the number 16 and replacing each X with 2.

$$16 + (4 \times 2) = 12 \times 2$$
$$16 + 8 = 24$$
$$24 = 24$$

Since each side of the equal sign (=) has the same value, equality has been preserved.

17. **a) A**

Step 1

Determine the equivalencies.

The diagram in this question compares the weight of two types of animals to that of a bear. On the first seesaw, 2 ponies = 1 bear; on the second seesaw, 3 tigers = 1 bear.

Given these equations, you can make the following inference: "Since 2 ponies and 3 tigers are equal to 1 bear, 2 ponies and 3 tigers should also be equal to each other."

Step 2

Work your way through each statement to determine which one is false.

Since 2 ponies = 3 tigers, the statement that two ponies are heavier than three tigers is false. Statement A is the false statement.

Calculate the number of ponies you need to balance 3 bears. Multiply 3 bears by 2 to get 6.

6 ponies = 3 bears

Therefore, 7 ponies are heavier than 3 bears. Statement B is true.

If 3 tigers = 1 bear and 2 ponies = 1 bear, then 3 tigers = 2 ponies. Statement C is true.

From the seesaws, 1 bear weighs the same as 2 ponies and the same as 3 tigers. Statement D is true.

18. **b) B**

Step 1

Determine the equivalencies of the three animals.

As shown in the given diagram, the weight of two ponies is equal to the weight of one bear.

2 ponies = 1 bear

The weight of three tigers is equal to the weight of one bear.

3 tigers = 1 bear

Because the weight of 2 ponies and the weight of 3 tigers are each equal to the weight of 1 bear, the weight of 2 ponies is equal to the weight of 3 tigers.

2 ponies = 3 tigers

Step 2

Calculate the number of tigers that would equal the weight of 6 ponies.

Multiply 2 ponies by 3 to equal 6 ponies. Also, multiply the number of tigers (3) by 3 to preserve equality.

$$2 \text{ ponies} \times 3 = 3 \text{ tigers} \times 3$$
$$6 \text{ ponies} = 9 \text{ tigers}$$

19. **c) A**

Step 1

Determine the equivalencies for the weights of the animals.

2 ponies = 1 bear
3 tigers = 1 bear
3 tigers = 2 ponies
9 tigers = 6 ponies

Step 2

Calculate how many tigers would be needed to balance the weight of 2 ponies and 2 bears.

Use the equivalencies to determine how many ponies are equal to 3 tigers.

2 ponies = 3 tigers

Since 1 bear = 3 tigers, multiply 1 bear by 2 and 3 tigers by 2 to calculate how many tigers are equal to 2 bears.

$$1 \text{ bear} \times 2 = 3 \text{ tigers} \times 2$$
$$2 \text{ bears} = 6 \text{ tigers}$$

Step 3

Add the number of tigers together.

$$3 + 6 = 9$$

Nine tigers are needed on the right side to balance the seesaw.

20. C

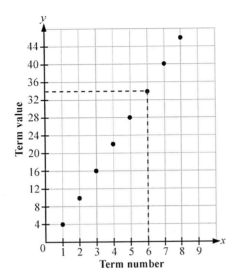

As shown in the graph, the term number that corresponds with the term value 34 is 6.

Shape and Space

SHAPE AND SPACE

Table of Correlations

Outcome		Practice Questions	Unit Test Questions	Sample PAT Part A	Sample PAT Part B
6SS1.0	Use direct and indirect measurement to solve problems.				
6SS1.1	Demonstrate an understanding of angles.	1, 2, 3	1, 2	*Part A of the PAT tests Number outcomes across grades 4, 5, and 6.*	11
6SS1.2	Demonstrate that the sum of interior angles is 180° in a triangle and 360° in a quadrilateral.	4, 5	3, 4		
6SS1.3	Develop and apply a formula for determining the perimeter of polygons, area of rectangles, and volume of right rectangular prisms.	6, 7	5, 6		12
6SS2.0	Describe the characteristics of 3-D objects and 2-D shapes, and analyze the relationships among them.				
6SS2.4	Construct and compare triangles in different orientations.	8, 9	7, 8		17
6SS2.5	Describe and compare the sides and angles of regular and irregular polygons.	10, 11	9, 10		18
6SS3.0	Describe and analyze position and motion of objects and shapes.				
6SS3.6	Perform a combination of translations, rotations and/or reflections on a single 2-D shape, with and without technology, and draw and describe the image.	12, 13, 14	11, 12		19
6SS3.7	Perform a combination of successive transformations of 2-D shapes to create a design, and identify and describe the transformations.	15, 16	13, 14		20
6SS3.8	Identify and plot points in the first quadrant of a Cartesian plane, using whole number ordered pairs.	17, 18	15, 16		21, 22
6SS3.9	Perform and describe single transformations of a 2-D shape in the first quadrant of a Cartesian plane.	19, 20	17, 18, 19		23, 24, 25

6SS1.1 Demonstrate an understanding of angles.

ANGLES

An **angle** is formed by two rays that share the same endpoint.

Angles are made up of three points. The name of the angle tells you the name of each point. For example, angle *WXY* is made up of three points: *W*, *X*, and *Y*.

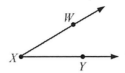

Angles are measured in degrees.

- An **acute angle** measures less than 90°.
- A **right angle** measures exactly 90°.
- An **obtuse angle** measures more than 90° but less than 180°.
- A **straight angle** measures exactly 180°.
- A **reflex angle** measures more than 180°.

Example

Jane draws four angles.

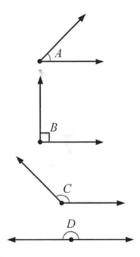

   Name angles *A*, *B*, *C*, and *D*. Justify your answer.

Solution

   Angle *A* is an acute angle because it is less than (<) 90°.

   Angle *B* is a right angle because it equals (=) 90°.

   Angle *C* is an obtuse angle because it is greater than (>) 90°.

   Angle *D* is a straight angle because it equals (=) 180°.

A protractor is a tool used to measure and construct angles.

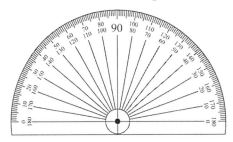

To measure an angle using a semicircular protractor, follow these steps:

1. Place the centre of the protractor on the vertex.
2. Line up the zero line of the protractor with the ray of the angle.
3. Use the proper scale to determine the degree of the angle. (Use the scale that starts at 0.)

Example

Jillian used a protractor to help her draw an angle.

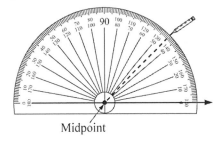

Midpoint

What is the measure of the angle Jillian drew? _____ °

Solution

Step 1

Starting at the 0° line, use the inner scale on the right side of the protractor, and count up the degrees by 10s to the number closest to the dotted line, but not crossing the line.
10°, 20°, 30°, 40°

Step 2

Since the dotted line is halfway between the 40° line and the 50° line, count the degrees by 1s to the halfway point, which is 45°.
41°, 42°, 43°, 44°, 45°
The measure of the angle Jillian drew is 45°.

To ensure accuracy, use a protractor when drawing an angle.

Example

Draw an angle that measures 145°.

Solution

Step 1

Draw the ray that will represent the zero line.

Step 2

Measure the angle.

Place the protractor on the ray so that the midpoint of the protractor lines up with the endpoint of the ray.

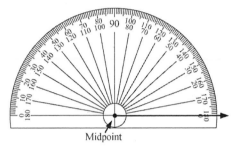

Midpoint

If the ray is pointing to the right, use the inside of the scale to make your measurement. If the ray is pointing to the left, use the outside scale. Always start measuring at 0°.

For this angle, the ray is pointing to the right, so use the inside scale.

Beginning at 0°, count 145°.

(10, 20 …140, 141, 142, 143, 144, 145)

Make a tick to mark the spot that shows 145°.

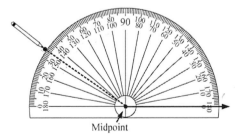

Midpoint

Step 3

Draw the angle.

Remove the protractor. Join the tick you marked (145°) to the endpoint of the original ray. Mark the angle with a small arc, and label the measurement.

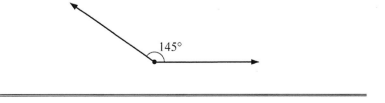

145°

Use the following information to answer the next question.

Korin uses a protractor to measure angle *C*, as shown in this diagram.

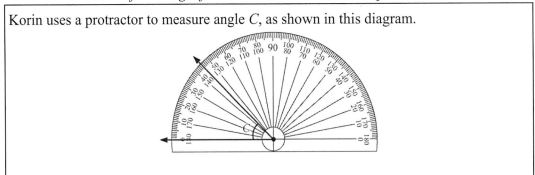

1. What is the measure of angle *C*?
   A. 45°   B. 56°
   C. 125°   D. 145°

Use the following information to answer the next question.

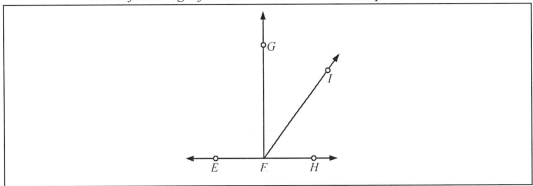

2. Which of the following statements about the given figure is **false**?
   A. Angle *HFE* is a straight angle.   B. Angle *EFG* is an obtuse angle.
   C. Angle *HFI* is an acute angle.   D. Angle *GFH* is a right angle.

Use the following information to answer the next question.

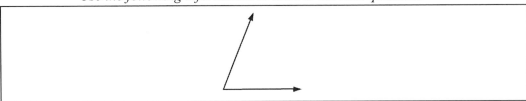

Numerical Response

3. The measure of the given angle is _____°.

6SS1.2   Demonstrate that the sum of interior angles is 180° in a triangle and 360° in a quadrilateral.

INTERIOR ANGLES

An **interior angle** is an angle inside a polygon. The interior angles of any triangle add up to 180°.

Example

Prove that the sum of the measures of all the interior angles of any triangle always equals 180°.

Solution

Step 1
Draw a number of different triangles.

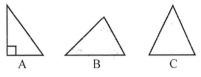

Step 2
Measure the angles.

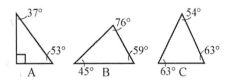

Step 3
Calculate the sum of the angles in each triangle.
Triangle A: 90° + 37° + 53° = 180°
Triangle B: 45° + 76° + 59° = 180°
Triangle C: 63° + 54° + 63° = 180°
No matter how the triangle is drawn, the sum is always 180°.

The interior angles of any quadrilateral add up to 360°.

Example

Find the sum of the angles of a quadrilateral.

Solution

Step 1

Draw any quadrilateral.

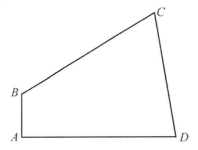

Step 2

Measure the angles.

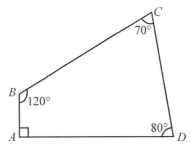

Step 3

Calculate the sum of the angles in the given quadrilateral.

$90° + 120° + 70° + 80° = 360°$

The sum of all the interior angles in any quadrilateral will always be 360°.

To find a missing interior angle, subtract the given angles from the total interior angles for the triangle or quadrilateral.

Example

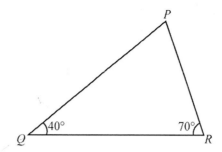

Angle *P* on triangle *PQR* is not labelled with a measure of degrees.

What is the measure of angle *P* in $\triangle PQR$?

Solution

Step 1
Identify the known angles.

$\triangle PQR$ has two known angles: $\angle Q = 40°$ and $\angle R = 70°$.

Step 2
Add the known angles.
$40° + 70° = 110°$

Step 3
Determine the missing measure.

A triangle's interior angles always add up to 180°. To find the missing angle, subtract the total of the known angles from 180°.
$180° - 110° = 70°$
$\qquad \angle P = 70°$

Use the following information to answer the next question.

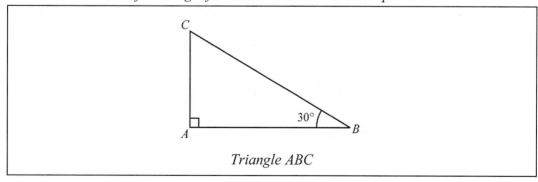

Triangle ABC

4. Given that triangle *ABC* is a right angle triangle, what is the value of angle *C*?

    A. 120°   **B.** 90°

    C. 60°   **D.** 30°

Use the following information to answer the next question.

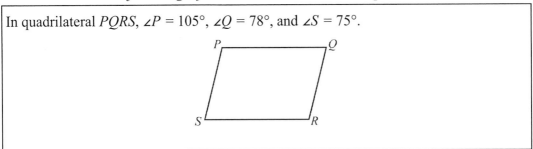

In quadrilateral *PQRS*, ∠*P* = 105°, ∠*Q* = 78°, and ∠*S* = 75°.

5. What is the measure of ∠*R*?
    A. 78°   B. 102°
    C. 120°   D. 160°

6SS1.3   Develop and apply a formula for determining the perimeter of polygons, area of rectangles, and volume of right rectangular prisms.

PERIMETER, AREA, AND VOLUME

Perimeter is the total distance around the outside edge of a polygon, like the distance around a yard. **Area** is the number of square units required to cover a surface, like tiles on a floor. **Volume** is the amount of space inside a prism, like the space inside a box.

PERIMETER OF POLYGONS

To determine the perimeter of a polygon, add all the side lengths together. For example, to determine the perimeter of a five-sided irregular polygon, use a formula like $P = s + s + s + s + s$ (Perimeter = side + side + side+side + side).

There are a few ways to determine the perimeter of a rectangle.

Example

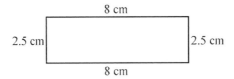

What is the perimeter of the given rectangle?

Solution

Method 1
There are several formulae that can be used to determine the perimeter of a rectangle (the distance all around a rectangle).

One formula is $P = l + w + l + w$
(Perimeter = length + width + length + width).
$P = 8 + 2.5 + 8 + 2.5 = 21$ cm

Method 2

Another formula for determining perimeter is $P = (2 \times l) + (2 \times w)$.

$P = (2 \times 8) + (2 \times 2.5)$
$\quad = 21$ cm

Sometimes this formula is written as $P = 2l + 2w$.

Method 3

Another formula for determining perimeter is $P = 2 \times (l + w)$ or

$P = 2 \times (8 + 2.5)$
$\quad = 21$ cm

Regardless of which perimeter formula you use, the perimeter of the given rectangle is 21 cm.

To determine the perimeter of a regular polygon, multiply the side length by the number of sides.

Recall that all the sides of a regular polygon are equal. For example, to determine the perimeter of a square, use a formula like $P = 4 \times s$.

Example

The playground in front of George's house is shaped like a regular pentagon. Each side of the playground is 10 m long.

What is the perimeter of the playground?

Solution

Method 1

To find the perimeter of a regular polygon, add up all the sides.

A pentagon has 5 sides, so $P = s + s + s + s + s$.

Each side is 10 m. Substitute 10 for s, and solve for P.

$P = s + s + s + s + s + s$
$\quad = 10 + 10 + 10 + 10 + 10$
$\quad = 50$ m

Method 2

Because the length of the sides of a pentagon are the same, you can multiply the length of one side by 5.

$P = 5 \times s$

Each side is 10 m. Substitute 10 for s, and solve for P.

$P = 5 \times s$

$\quad = 5 \times 10$

$\quad = 50$ m

The perimeter of the playground is 50 m.

AREA OF RECTANGLES

To calculate the area of a rectangle, multiply the length by the width: $A = l \times w$.

Example

The floor of a room is covered by eight square tiles. Each square tile has a side length of 4 m.

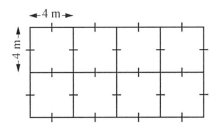

What is the total area of the tiled floor?

Solution

Step 1

Determine the length and width of the tiled floor.

The length of the tiled floor is 16 m.
$4 \text{ m} \times 4 = 16 \text{ m}$

The width of the tiled floor is 8 m.
$4 \text{ m} \times 2 = 8 \text{ m}$

Step 2

Calculate the area of the tiled floor.

$$\begin{aligned} A &= l \times w \\ &= 16 \times 8 \\ &= 128 \text{ m}^2 \end{aligned}$$

The total area of the tiled floor is 128 m^2.

VOLUME OF RIGHT RECTANGULAR PRISMS

Volume can be determined by filling the prism with same-size cubes. The number of cubes used to completely fill the length, width, and height of the prism is the volume.

Volume is measured in cubic units, or units^3.

One way to determine the volume using a formula is to multiply the length of the base by the width of the base by the height of the prism. $V = l \times w \times h$

Another way to determine the volume using a formula is to first determine the area of the base ($l \times w$), and then multiply the area by the height of the prism.
$$V_{\text{rectangular prism}} = A_{\text{base}} \times h$$

Example

Jari uses cubic units to measure the volume of this rectangular prism.

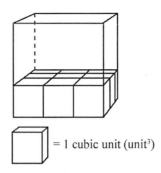

= 1 cubic unit (unit³)

When Jari fills the rectangular prism to the top with cubic units, what will be the volume of the prism?

Solution

Step 1

To determine the area of the base, count the number of cubic units needed to cover the base. (1, 2, 3 ... 9)

You can also use the area formula to determine the area of the base by multiplying the length (3 cubic units) by the width (3 cubic units).

$A = l \times w$
$\quad = 3 \times 3$
$\quad = 9$

The area of the base is 9 units³.

Step 2

Based on the size of the cubic units, two more layers of cubes will be needed to fill the rectangular prism. That means that the height of the prism will be 3 cubic units.

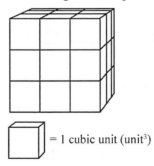

= 1 cubic unit (unit³)

To determine the volume, multiply the area of the base (9 units³) by the height (3 units³).

$V = A_{base} \times h$
$\quad = 9 \times 3$
$\quad = 27$ units³

The given rectangular prism will have a volume of 27 units³.

6. If a rectangle is 3 cm long and 2.5 cm wide, what is its perimeter?
   A. 5.5 cm   B. 7.5 cm
   C. 11.0 cm   D. 15.0 cm

7. How many times larger will the area of rectangle *M* be than the area of rectangle *A*?
   A. 6 times larger   B. 5 times larger
   C. 4 times larger   D. 3 times larger

6SS2.4   Construct and compare triangles in different orientations.

TRIANGLES

All triangles are composed of three sides and three angles. The angles in a triangle are called interior angles.

Triangles can be classified according to the measure of their interior angles and side lengths.

This diagram shows a triangle with three different side lengths and three different angle measures.

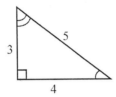

CLASSIFYING TRIANGLES

An **acute triangle** has three acute angles. An acute angle is less than 90°.

Example
   Three angles are given for the triangle shown.

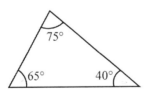

   Based on its angles, classify the given triangle.

Solution

   A triangle that has each of the three interior angles measuring less than 90° is called an acute triangle.

   Since the angles in the given triangle are all less than 90° (75°, 65°, and 45°), the given triangle is classified as an acute triangle.

A **right triangle** has one right angle of 90°.

Example

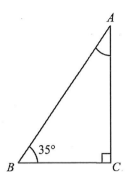

Based on its angles, classify triangle *ABC*.

Solution

Step 1

Identify the angle measures.

Angle *B* has a given measure of 35°. Angle *C* has a measure of 90°, as indicated by the square corner. Angle A does not have a given measure, but it is an acute angle, so the measure is less than 90°.

Step 2

Classify triangle *ABC*.

Recall that any triangle that has an angle measuring 90° is classified as a right-angled triangle or a right triangle.

Since angle *C* has a measure of 90°, triangle *ABC* is classified as a right triangle.

An **obtuse triangle** has one obtuse angle. An obtuse angle is greater than 90° and less than 180°.

Example

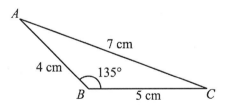

Triangle *ABC* is shown with several measurements given.

Based on its angles, classify triangle *ABC*.

Solution

A triangle in which one of the angles measures more than 90° but less than 180° is called an obtuse triangle.

In triangle *ABC*, angle *B* is more than 90° but less than 180°: $\angle ABC = 135°$.

Triangle *ABC* is classified as an obtuse triangle.

An **isosceles triangle** has two equal sides and two equal angles.

Example

Three sides are given for triangle *ABC*, as shown.

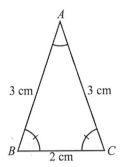

Based on its sides and angles, classify triangle *ABC*.

Solution

If two sides of a triangle are equal, the triangle is called an isosceles triangle. If two interior angles have the same measure, the triangle is called an isosceles triangle.

For triangle *ABC*, side *AB* and side *AC* are equal.
$AB = AC = 3$ cm

Angle *B* and angle *C* are equal as shown by the marking on the angle arc.

Triangle *ABC* is an isosceles triangle.

An **equilateral triangle** has three equal sides and three equal angles.

Example

The illustration shows triangle *ABC* in which $AB = AC = BC$.

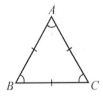

Based on its angles, classify triangle *ABC*.

Solution

For triangle *ABC*, the three line segments are equal $AB = AC = BC$. If the three line segments are equal then the three angles are also equal. A triangle that has three equal angles is classified as an equilateral triangle.

Triangle *ABC* is classified as an equilateral triangle.

A **scalene triangle** has no equal sides and no equal angles.

Example

Ricky drew this triangle with sides measuring 4 cm, 6 cm, and 8 cm.

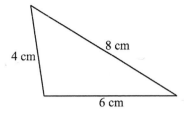

What type of triangle can Ricky's triangle be classified as?

Solution

A triangle that has no equal sides and no equal angles is called a scalene triangle.

The sides of Ricky's triangle are all different lengths.

Therefore, Ricky's triangle is classified as a scalene triangle.

DRAWING TRIANGLES

In order to accurately draw a triangle, you need a protractor and a ruler. Use the protractor to measure out the exact angle or angles you require. Use the ruler to measure out the exact side lengths.

Example

Draw an isosceles triangle with a base measuring 4 cm and two congruent angles of 45°.

Solution

Step 1
Draw the base.

Using a centimetre ruler, draw a line segment that is 4 cm long.

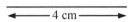

Step 2
Construct the two angles.

At one endpoint of the line segment, construct a 45° angle using a protractor.

At the other endpoint of the line segment, construct another 45° angle using a protractor.

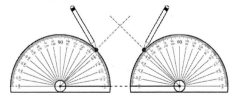

Step 3

Construct the third angle.

The two rays of the constructed angles will intersect to form the third angle of the triangle. Since the total number of degrees in any triangle is 180°, the measure of the third angle is 90°.

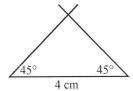

Erase the excess from the triangle. Your completed isosceles triangle should look like this.

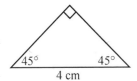

In order to replicate a given triangle in a different orientation, draw or trace the triangle in a different position. Remember, for the triangles to be congruent, the side measures and angle measures must be identical. Only the position can change.

Example

Draw the illustrated triangle in three different orientations.

Solution

Step 1

Measure the sides of the given triangle.

The triangle has three sides that each measure 1 cm, making it an equilateral triangle. The triangles you draw must all have 1 cm side lengths.

Step 2

Replicate the triangle in different orientations.

Draw three 1 cm equilateral triangles that are in different positions.

There are many positions or orientations you can draw.

Here are three replicated triangles.

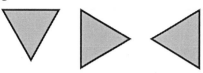

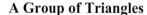

Use the following information to answer the next question.

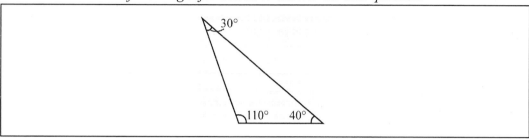

8.   The word used to describe the type of triangle shown in the diagram is
   A. equilateral   **B.** obtuse

   C. acute   **D.** right

Use the following information to answer the next question.

The teacher drew these four triangles on the whiteboard.

A Group of Triangles

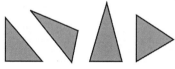

9.   The given triangles are similar because they all have one or more
   A. right angles   **B.** acute angles

   C. obtuse angles   **D.** straight angles

6SS2.5   Describe and compare the sides and angles of regular and irregular polygons.

REGULAR AND IRREGULAR POLYGONS

A **polygon** is a closed 2-D shape with three or more straight sides.

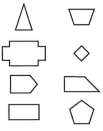

A **regular polygon** has all congruent sides and angles.

An **irregular polygon** is any other polygon whose sides and angles are not all congruent.

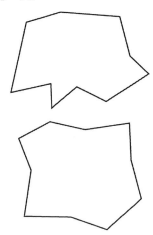

2-D shapes can be sorted by these properties:

• Whether they are polygons or non-polygons
• Size of the corresponding angles
• Length of the corresponding sides

When two polygons are identical, they are called **congruent**. To check for congruency, you can superimpose the two images, putting them on top of one another, or you can measure their sides and angles.

Example

Five triangles are given.

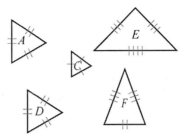

Which triangle is congruent to triangle *A*?

Solution

When one shape is congruent to another, the size and shape are exactly the same.

Trace triangle *A* onto a piece of paper and cut it out. Then, place it over the other triangles to see which one matches up with it exactly. Upon completing this procedure, you will notice that triangle *D* is congruent to triangle *A* because it is the same size and shape as triangle *A*.

Use the following information to answer the next question.

10. Which of the given figures is a polygon?
    A. I   **B.** II
    C. III   **D.** IV

11. Which of the following shapes is **not** a polygon?
    A. Circle   **B.** Square
    C. Triangle   **D.** Rectangle

6SS3.6   Perform a combination of translations, rotations and/or reflections on a single 2-D shape, with and without technology, and draw and describe the image.

TRANSFORMATIONS OF 2-D SHAPES

A **transformation** is a movement of a shape without changing its size or shape. The original shape and the transformation are always congruent.

Transformations include translations (slides), reflections (flips), and rotations (turns).

In a **reflection**, the transformation takes on a mirror image of the original shape. Both the position and location of the shape changes.

In a **translation**, the sides of the original shape and the image are parallel to each other. Only the position of the shape changes.

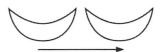

In a **rotation**, the vertices of the original shape move the same distance from the rotation point as the vertices of the rotated image. Both the position and location of the shape can change.

A combination of transformations can take place.

When describing transformations, describe the horizontal transformation first and then the vertical transformation.

When performing transformations, perform each transformation separately to achieve the desired new image.

Example

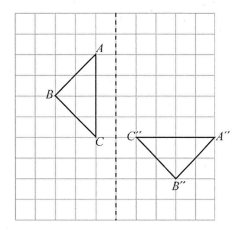

A student transformed figure *ABC* to figure *A″B″C″*.

Explain the two transformations needed for figure *ABC* to move to the position shown by figure *A″B″C″*.

Solution

Step 1

Determine the first transformation.

The first transformation is a rotation.

In order for figure *ABC* to be on the same horizontal line as figure *A″B″C″*, figure *ABC* needs to rotate 90° counterclockwise around vertex *C*.

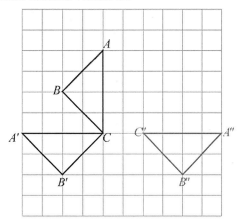

Step 2

Determine the second transformation.

The second transformation is a reflection.

Figure *A'B'C* is one square to the left of the line of reflection. When the figure is flipped one square to the right of the line of reflection, it will take the position of figure *A"B"C"*.

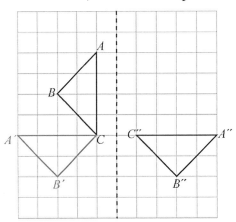

Example

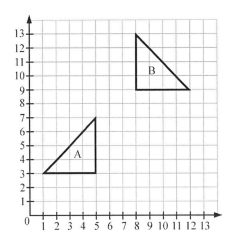

What transformations must happen to move the triangle from position A to position B?

Solution

Remember to describe transformations horizontally and then vertically.

Step 1

Determine the coordinates of the triangle in position A.

- The coordinates of the bottom left corner of the triangle are (1, 3).
- The coordinates of the bottom right corner of the triangle are (5, 3).
- The coordinates of the top right corner of the triangle are (5, 7).

Step 2

Move the triangle from position A three squares to the right.

Starting at the bottom left corner of the triangle and moving horizontally and then vertically, the new coordinates of the triangle in position A' will be (4, 3), (8, 3), and (8, 7).

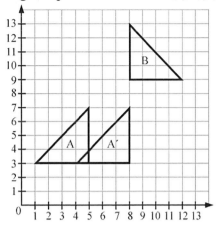

Step 3

Move the triangle up six squares.

Starting at the bottom left corner of the triangle and moving horizontally and then vertically, the new coordinates of the triangle in position A" will be (4, 9), (8, 9), and (8, 13).

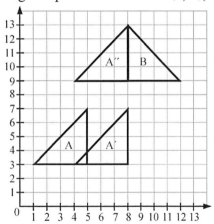

Step 4

Flip the triangle over the vertical line to move the triangle into position B.

The coordinates are (8, 9), (12, 9), and (8, 13).

Use the following information to answer the next question.

The teacher draws this figure on the whiteboard.

12. If the given figure is flipped twice across a horizontal axis, which of the following figures shows the new position?

A.

B.

C.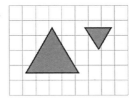

D.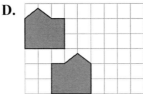

13. Which of the following pairs of figures shows a translation?

A.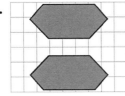

B.

C.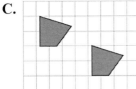

D.

14. Which of the following transformations turns the letter **N** into a **Z**?
   A. A diagonal translation
   B. A reflection across a flip line
   C. A 90° rotation around the centre
   D. A 180° rotation around the centre

6SS3.7 Perform a combination of successive transformations of 2-D shapes to create a design, and identify and describe the transformations.

CREATING DESIGNS WITH 2-D SHAPES

Some designs are made by successively transforming one or more 2-D shapes. The design needs to be examined carefully in order to identify the original shape and the transformations used to create the design.

Example

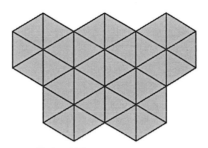

The given image was created through transformations.

What transformations took place to create this design?

Solution

Step 1
Identify the original shape used to create the design.

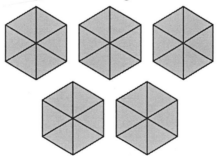

Separate the given design into parts to find the starting shape.

Five hexagons were used to make the design.

Each hexagon shape is made out of rotated triangles.

The starting shape of the design is a triangle.

Step 2

Identify the transformations that took place.

There were two transformations that took place.

A triangle was rotated to create the hexagon shape.

The hexagon shapes could be described as translations or reflections.

In this diagram, arrows have been used to show one way that the directions of the slides could have occurred.

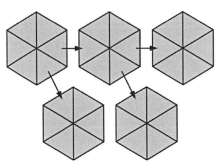

In this diagram, mirror lines have been inserted to show one way that the flips could have occurred.

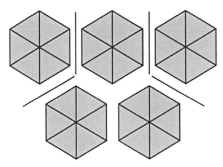

---

15. Which of the following letter designs was created by using flips?

A. **MWMWMW**

B. **S S S S S S S**

C. **Q̇ ȯ ̇o ȯ**

D. **qpqpqp**

16. Which of the following designs shows a horizontal slide?

A.
B.

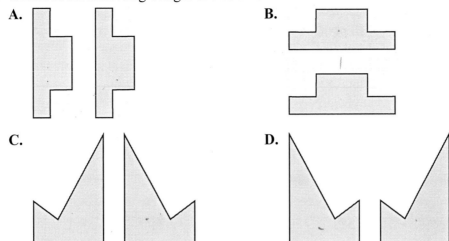

C.
D.

6SS3.8   Identify and plot points in the first quadrant of a Cartesian plane, using whole number ordered pairs.

THE CARTESIAN PLANE

The Cartesian plane or coordinate system is a method of assigning a pair of numbers to each point on a plane. Each pair of numbers uniquely describes the point's position.

Example

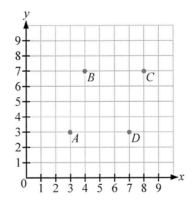

Write the coordinates for the given plotted points.

Solution

Step 1

Find the coordinates for the plotted points along the x-axis.

Start at the origin (0, 0) for all plotted points. Move along the x-axis (horizontal axis) to find the first number of each ordered pair.

- Point A is located at 3 along the x-axis.
- Point B is located at 4 along the x-axis.
- Point C is located at 8 along the x-axis.
- Point D is located at 7 along the x-axis.

Step 2

Find the coordinates for the plotted points along the *y*-axis.

Start at the origin (0, 0) for all plotted points. Move along the *y*-axis (vertical axis) to find the second number of each ordered pair.

- Point *A* is located at 3 along the *y*-axis.
- Point *B* is located at 7 along the *y*-axis.
- Point *C* is located at 7 along the *y*-axis.
- Point *D* is located at 3 along the *y*-axis.

Step 3

Write the ordered pair for the plotted points.

Take the point locations on the *x*- and *y*-axis, and write each as an ordered pair. Be sure to list the horizontal coordinate (*x*-axis) first and the vertical coordinate (*y*-axis) second (*x*, *y*).

- Point *A* (3, 3)
- Point *B* (4, 7)
- Point *C* (8, 7)
- Point *D* (7, 3)

You can plot a point on the Cartesian plane if you are given the point's coordinates.

Look at the ordered pair, and find out where along the *x*- and *y*-axes the point is located. Make sure you start at the point of origin (0, 0) before counting your moves on the Cartesian plane.

Not all Cartesian planes have axes with number intervals of one. Some increase by twos, some by fives, and some even by tens.

Example

Locate the coordinates (2, 2), (3, 4), and (4, 2) in the first quadrant of a Cartesian plane.

Solution

Step 1

Identify the location of (2, 2) on the Cartesian plane.

Trace your finger along the *x*-axis until you get to 2. Then, trace your finger up the *y*-axis until you get to 2. The point where the 2 on the *x*-axis and the 2 on the *y*-axis meet is where this coordinate point is located.

Step 2

Identify the location of (3, 4) on the Cartesian plane.

Move along the *x*-axis until you get to 3. Then, move up the *y*-axis until you get to 4. The point where the 3 on the *x*-axis and the 4 on the *y*-axis meet is where this coordinate point is located.

Step 3

Identify the location of (4, 2) on the Cartesian plane.

Move along the *x*-axis until you get to 4. Then, move up the *y*-axis until you get to 2. The point where the 4 on the *x*-axis and the 2 on the *y*-axis meet is where this coordinate point is located.

The points can be plotted in the first quadrant of the Cartesian plane as shown on the given diagram.

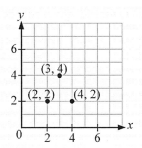

Given the coordinates of the vertices, a 2-D shape can be drawn on a Cartesian plane.

Example

Points *A*(1, 7), *B*(2, 3), *C*(7, 3), and *D*(6, 7) are plotted on a Cartesian plane and connected with line segments.

Draw and identify the shape formed from the given coordinates.

Solution

Step 1

Draw all four points in quadrant I on the Cartesian plane, and connect the plotted points with line segments.

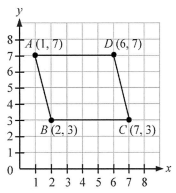

Step 2

Identify the shape.

Line segments *AB* and *CD* are parallel and equal in length. Also, line segments *AD* and *BC* are parallel and equal in length. The shape formed is a parallelogram.

Use the following information to answer the next question.

Robert plotted three points on a graph using the ordered pairs (3, 4), (7, 2), and (6, 6). Then, he connected the points with line segments to create a design.

17. Which of the following designs did Robert make when he plotted the given points and drew the line segments?

A.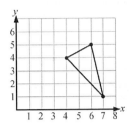

B.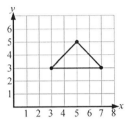

C.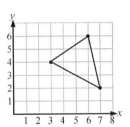

D.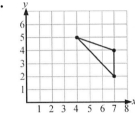

Use the following information to answer the next question.

Here is a set of coordinates.

$$(1, 4), (2, 5), (3, 7), (4, 11)$$

18. Which of the following graphs shows the given set of coordinates plotted correctly?

A.

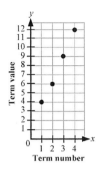

B.

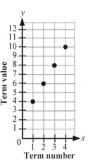

C.

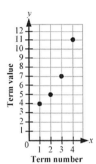

D.

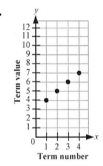

6SS3.9 *Perform and describe single transformations of a 2-D shape in the first quadrant of a Cartesian plane.*

TRANSFORMATIONS ON A CARTESIAN PLANE

A Cartesian plane can be used to perform a transformation of a given 2-D shape. The transformation can be described by counting the number of squares the shape moved from one position to another position.

Example

Sean drew a square on the coordinate grid in position A. He then translated the shape to position B.

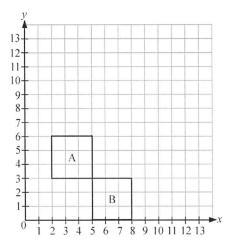

Describe the transformation that moved the square from position A to position B.

Solution

Step 1

Count the number of squares that the square moved to the right (horizontally).

It moved 3 squares to the right.

Step 2

Count the number of squares that the square moved down (vertically).

It moved 3 squares down.

Step 3

Describe the transformation.

The transformation of the square from position A to B is a slide of 3 to the right and 3 down.

Use the following information to answer the next question.

Julianna plots five points on a grid and then joins all the points to make this design.

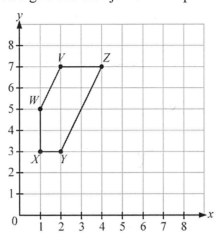

19. If Julianna flips the shape so that point *Z* remains in the same position, then the coordinates of points *W* and *Y* will be

    A. *W*(8, 5) and *Y*(5, 3)   **B.** *W*(7, 5) and *Y*(6, 3)

    C. *W*(5, 7) and *Y*(3, 6)   **D.** *W*(1, 5) and *Y*(2, 3)

Use the following information to answer the next question.

The given grid shows the transformation of a triangle from Position 1 to Position 2.

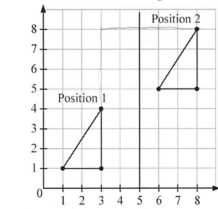

20. Which of the following transformations was used to move the triangle from Position 1 to Position 2?

    A. Slide 5 to the right and 4 up.   **B.** Slide 4 to the right and 5 up.

    C. Slide 4 to the right and 3 up.   **D.** Slide 3 to the right and 4 up.

ANSWERS AND SOLUTIONS
SHAPE AND SPACE

1. A	5. B	9. B	13. C	17. C
2. B	6. C	10. C	14. C	18. C
3. 68	7. C	11. A	15. D	19. B
4. C	8. B	12. A	16. A	20. A

1. A

The centre point of the protractor is lined up with the vertex of angle C (where the two rays of the angle meet). The bottom ray of the angle is lined up with the $0°$ mark on the left side of the protractor.

Since the given angle faces the left side of the protractor, it needs to be read starting with the $0°$ mark on the outer part of the scale on the left side.
Starting at $0°$, count the degrees up to the tick at which the other ray of the angle crosses the scale.
10, 20, 30, 40, 41, 42, 43, 44, 45

The measure of angle C is $45°$.

2. B

Step 1
Recall the measures of the angles in the options.

- Right angles have a measure of $90°$.
- Acute angles have a measure less than $90°$.
- Obtuse angles have a measure greater than $90°$ and less than $180°$.
- Straight angles have a measure of $180°$.

Step 2
Identify the incorrect statement.
The incorrect statement is that angle EFG is an obtuse angle.
Since angle EFG forms a square corner, it has a measure of $90°$, which makes it a right angle.To be an obtuse angle, it would need to have a measure that is greater than $90°$ and less than $180°$, like angle EFI.

3. 68

HINT: Since the given angle is less than a right angle, then you know the given angle will be less than $90°$.

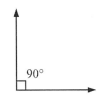

Step 1
First, place your protractor on the bottom ray so that the midpoint lines up with the vertex of the angle.
Start at the right side of the protractor's inner scale at the $0°$ line, and count by 10s until you reach the number of degrees closest to the upper ray without passing it.
$10°, 20°, 30°…60°$

Step 2
Next, count the individual ticks after $60°$ by 1s until you reach the upper ray of the angle.
$…61°, 62°, 63°…68°$

The measure of the given angle is $68°$.

4. C

Step 1
Calculate the sum of angle A and angle B.
$30° + 90° = 120°$

Step 2
Calculate the measure of angle C.
Subtract the sum of angle A and angle B from $180°$ to find the measure of angle C.
$180° − 120° = 60°$
Angle C is $60°$.

5. **B**

Step 1

Identify the total sum of all the angles of a quadrilateral.

The sum of all the angles of any quadrilateral is $360°$.

$\angle P + \angle S + \angle Q + \angle R = 360°$

Step 2

Substitute the values in and solve for angle R.

Angle P is $105°$, angle S is $75°$, and angle Q is $78°$.

$105° + 75° + 78° + R = 360°$
$258° + R = 360°$
$R = 360° - 258°$
$R = 102°$

Angle R is $102°$.

6. **C**

To determine the perimeter, add the two equal side lengths and the two equal side widths that make up the four sides of the rectangle.

$P = l + w + l + w$
$P = 3 + 2.5 + 3 + 2.5$
$P = 11.0 \text{ cm}$

The perimeter of the rectangle is 11.0 cm.

7. **C**

Step 1

Determine the length and width of rectangle A. The length is 2 units, and the width is 3 units.

$A = l \times w$
$A = 2 \times 3$
$A = 6 \text{ units}^2$

Step 2

Double the length and width of rectangle A to determine the length and width of rectangle M.

Length: $2 \times 2 = 4$ units
Width: $3 \times 2 = 6$ units

Step 3

Use the area formula to determine the area of rectangle M.

$A = l \times w$
$A = 4 \times 6$
$A = 24 \text{ units}^2$

Step 4

To determine how many times larger the area of rectangle M is than rectangle A, divide the area of rectangle M by the area of rectangle A.

$\dfrac{24}{6} = 4$

The area of rectangle M will be 4 times larger than the area of rectangle A.

8. **B**

An obtuse angle has a measure greater than $90°$.

Since one of the angles in this triangle is $110°$, it is classified as an obtuse triangle or an obtuse-angled triangle.

9. **B**

Step 1

Examine each triangle to identify the types of angles it contains.

- The first triangle has one right angle ($90°$) and two acute angles ($< 90°$).
- The second triangle has one obtuse angle ($> 90°$) and two acute angles ($< 90°$).
- The last two triangles each have three acute angles ($< 90°$).

Step 2

Determine which type of angle is found in all four of the triangles.

The four triangles are similar because they all have one or more acute angles.

10. **C**

A polygon is a closed figure formed by line segments where each line segment intersects exactly two other line segments.

Figure I is not a polygon because it is not formed by line segments only. Figure II is not a polygon because it is not a closed figure. Figure IV is not a polygon because some of its sides do not intersect exactly two other line segments.

Figure III meets all the criteria in the definition of a polygon; therefore, figure III is a polygon.

11. **A**

A polygon is a plane figure having three or more sides. A circle has neither sides nor vertices; therefore, a circle is not a polygon.

12. A

Step 1

Determine the line of reflection.

The line of reflection is a horizontal axis. This is how the figure will look after the first flip.

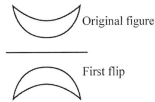

Step 2

Flip the figure a second time. This is how the figure will look after the second flip.

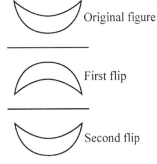

After the second flip, the figure will look exactly the same as it did originally.

13. C

A translation occurs when a figure slides from its original position to a new position. Nothing else changes in a translation except the location. The figure will look exactly the same as it did in its original position.

This pair of figures shows a translation.

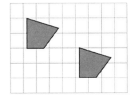

The translation shown can be described as moving to the right (→) and then moving down (↓). It can also be described as moving diagonally (↘).

14. C

To change the letter **N** into the letter **Z**, it must be rotated 90°. The rotation can be either clockwise or counterclockwise. Both rotations will turn the N into a Z.

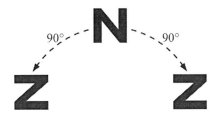

15. D

A flip is a transformation where a figure is flipped or reflected across a line, creating a mirror image of the original figure.

This letter design

ꟼPꟼPꟼP

Was created by flipping the letter P five times across vertical flip lines.

16. A

A slide (translation) occurs when a figure moves from its original position to a new position, without any changes made to the figure. A horizontal slide is one that moves to the left or to the right.

This design shows a horizontal slide that slid to the right.

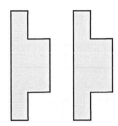

The shape of the second figure is identical in all aspects to the shape of the first figure.

17. C

Step 1

Plot the given ordered pairs on the graph.
(3, 4), (7, 2), (6, 6)

The first number of the ordered pair (to the left of the comma) is located on the *x*-axis.

The second number of the ordered pair (to the right of the comma) is located on the *y*-axis.

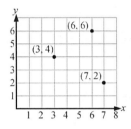

Step 2

Connect the points with line segments.

This graph shows the design that Robert created when he plotted the given points and connected them with line segments.

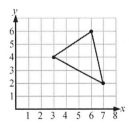

18. C

The *x*-coordinate is the term number, which is the first number in each ordered pair of coordinates. The *y*-coordinate is the corresponding term value, which is the second number in each ordered pair of coordinates.

Follow these directions as you check to see which graph has the coordinates plotted correctly:

1. For each coordinate, start at 0 and move to the right on the *x*-axis until you reach the term number you are looking for.
2. Move vertically until you reach the line that the corresponding term value from the *y*-axis is on.
3. The coordinate will be located where the two lines intersect.

This graph shows the given coordinates plotted correctly.

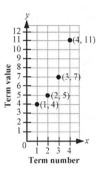

19. B

This diagram shows what the coordinates of the shape will be when the figure is flipped so that point *Z* remains in the same position, which is (4, 7).

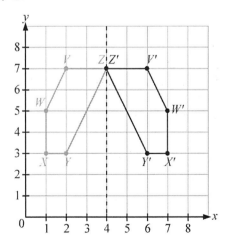

- After the flip, the coordinates of point *W* will be (7, 5).
- After the flip, the coordinates of point *Y* will be (6, 3).

After Julianna flips the shape, the coordinates for *W* and *Y* will be *W* (7, 5) and *Y* (6, 3).

20. **A**

Step 1

If you slide the triangle 5 squares to the right, the right angle will have the coordinates (8, 1).

Step 2

If you then slide the triangle up 4 squares, the right angle will have the coordinates (8, 5), which are the same coordinates for the right angle of the triangle in Position 2.

The transformation of sliding 5 to the right and 4 up was used to move the triangle from Position 1 to 2.

UNIT TEST — SHAPE AND SPACE

Use the following information to answer the next question.

Harry used a protractor to draw these angles.

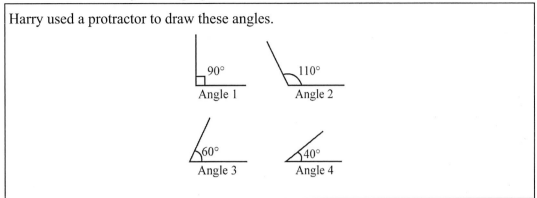

1. Which of the angles that Harry drew is an obtuse angle?
   A. Angle 1   B. Angle 2
   C. Angle 3   D. Angle 4

2. Which of the following angles is labelled correctly?
   A. Obtuse angle   B. Acute angle

   C. Straight angle   D. Right angle

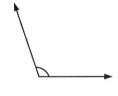   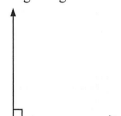

3. According to the given measures, which of the following triangles is **not** correctly constructed?

   A.   B.

   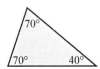

   C.   D.

Use the following information to answer the next question.

The school playground in the given figure is in the form of a quadrilateral.

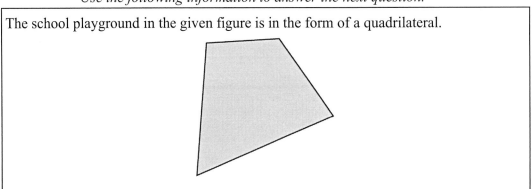

4. What is the sum of the interior angles of the playground?
    A. 270°   **B.** 360°
    C. 450°   **D.** 540°

Use the following information to answer the next question.

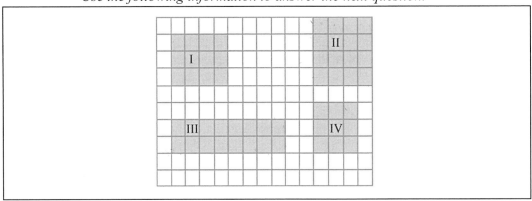

5. Which of the given rectangles has a perimeter of 16 units and an area of 16 units^2?
    A. Rectangle I   **B.** Rectangle II
    C. Rectangle III   **D.** Rectangle IV

Use the following information to answer the next question.

The diagram shows the dimensions of a box for a board game.

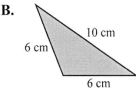

60 cm

3 cm

20 cm

6. If 5 board games of this size can be packed into a crate, the minimum volume of the crate must be

A. 3 600 cm³ **B.** 10 800 cm³

C. 14 400 cm³ **D.** 18 000 cm³

Use the following information to answer the next question.

A triangle is given.

70°

72° 38°

7. This triangle is

A. a right triangle **B.** a scalene triangle

C. an obtuse triangle **D.** an isosceles triangle

8. Which of the following triangles is an isosceles triangle?

A.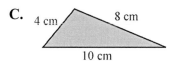

7 cm 8 cm

6 cm

B.

10 cm

6 cm

6 cm

C.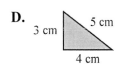

4 cm 8 cm

10 cm

D.

3 cm 5 cm

4 cm

9. A polygon is said to be regular when
   A. all its sides and angles are equal

   B. neither its sides nor its angles are equal

   C. its angles are equal but all its sides are not

   D. its sides are equal but all its angles are not

10. Which of the following polygons is irregular?

    A.   B.

    C.   D.

11. Which of the following pairs of figures shows a rotation?

    A. 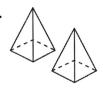   B.

    C. 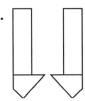   D.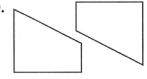

Use the following information to answer the next question.

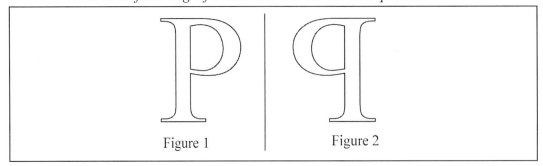

Figure 1   Figure 2

12. Which of the following transformations occurred to change figure 1 into figure 2?
    A. Turn   B. Slide
    C. Reflection   D. Translation

13. Which of the following tiling patterns can be obtained by performing a series of translations and reflections?

A.

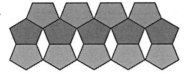

B.

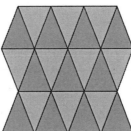

C.

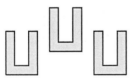

D.

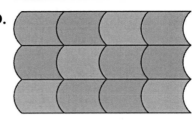

Use the following information to answer the next question.

In art class, Marnie used this block letter to create different designs.

14. Which of the following designs was created by translating the letter?

A.

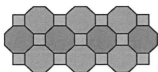

B.

C.

D.

Use the following information to answer the next question.

Don wants to plot the coordinates $P(3, 3)$, $Q(2, 6)$, $R(7, 7)$, and $S(5, 5)$ in the first quadrant of this Cartesian plane.

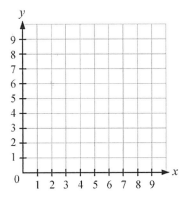

15. When the coordinates are joined by lines, what shape will Don have made?

    A. Kite   **B.** Square

    C. Triangle   **D.** Parallelogram

Use the following information to answer the next question.

Marcy uses these coordinates to draw a design on a grid: $(0, 1)$, $(5, 2)$, $(4, 5)$, and $(1, 4)$.

16. Which of the following designs did Marcy draw?

    A.

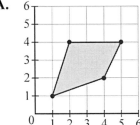

    B.

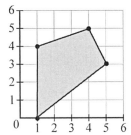

    C.

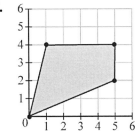

    D.

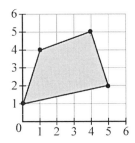

Use the following information to answer the next question.

This graph shows the transformation of a figure from position *A* to position *B*.

17. Which of the following transformations will move the figure from position *A* to position *B*?

    A. Slide down one, flip vertically, then slide right two.

    B. Flip vertically, slide right two, then slide down one.

    C. Slide right one, slide down two, then flip vertically.

    D. Flip vertically, slide right one, then slide down two.

Use the following information to answer the next question.

The given images show a series of transformations from the original image to image 2.

Original shape   Image 1   Image 2

18. Which of the following series of transformations occurred between the original image, image 1, and image 2?

    A. A 90° counterclockwise rotation and then a translation

    B. A reflection and then a 90° counterclockwise rotation

    C. A 90° clockwise rotation and then a translation

    D. A reflection and then a 90° clockwise rotation

Use the following information to answer the next question.

Rectangle $W'X'Y'Z'$ was drawn after a 90° counterclockwise rotation about the point $(5, 4)$.

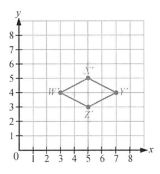

Written Response

19. Draw the original rectangle $WXYZ$.

ANSWERS AND SOLUTIONS — UNIT TEST

1. B	6. D	11. D	16. D
2. D	7. B	12. C	17. D
3. B	8. B	13. B	18. D
4. B	9. A	14. C	19. WR
5. B	10. C	15. C	

1. B

An obtuse angle is an angle that has a measure that is greater than 90° (a right angle) and less than a 180° angle (a straight line).
Angle 2 has a measure of 110°, which is *greater* than 90° and *less* than 180°.
90° < 110° < 180°

Angle 2 is an obtuse angle.

2. D

This diagram shows a 90° angle, which forms a square corner where the two perpendicular rays meet. These angles are classified as right angles.

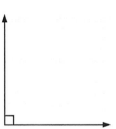

3. B

The sum of the three angles of a triangle must add up to 180 degrees to be correctly constructed.

70° + 70° + 40° = 180° The triangle is correctly constructed.

50° + 90° + 40° = 180° The triangle is correctly constructed.

50° + 60° + 70° = 180° The triangle is correctly constructed.

60° + 100° + 30° = 190° The triangle is incorrectly constructed.

4. B

The sum of the interior angles of any quadrilateral is 360°.

5. B

Step 1

Count the number of units across→ to determine the lengths of the given rectangles. Count the number of units upward↑ to determine the widths of the given rectangles.

Step 2

Use a perimeter formula like $P = 2 \times (l + w)$ to determine the perimeters of the given rectangles.

Use the area formula $A = l \times w$ to determine the areas of the given rectangles.

Substitute the appropriate numbers for the lengths and widths in the formulas.

Step 3

Rectangle II:

$P = 2 \times (l + w)$
$P = 2 \times (4 + 4)$
$P = 16$ units
$A = l \times w$
$A = 4 \times 4$
$A = 16$ units^2

Rectangle II has a perimeter of 16 units and an area of 16 units^2.

6. D

Step 1

First, determine the volume of one board game by multiplying the length (20 cm) by the width (60 cm) by the height (3 cm).

$V = l \times w \times h$
$V = 20 \times 60 \times 3 = 3\ 600$ cm^3

Step 2

To determine the minimum volume of a crate that can hold 5 board games, multiply the volume of one game by 5.

$3\ 600 \times 5 = 18\ 000$ cm^3

The minimum volume of the crate would be 18 000 cm^3.

7. B

Step1

Examine the angle measures.

Each angle has a different measure. One angle is 72°, one is 70°, and one is 38°.

Step 2

Identify the name of the triangle.

Recall that a triangle with three different side lengths and three different angle measures is a scalene triangle.

Since all three angles of the given triangle have different measures, the triangle is a scalene triangle.

8. B

Step 1

Recall the characteristics of an isosceles triangle.

An isosceles triangle has two equal side lengths and two equal interior angles.

Step 2

Identify the isosceles triangle.

The triangles in the alternatives do not show the measures of the angles, but the measures of the side lengths are given.

This triangle has two side lengths that are 6 cm long.

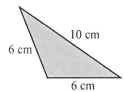

It is an isosceles triangle.

9. A

The definition of a regular polygon is that it contains sides of equal length and angles of equal measure.

10. C

A polygon with three or more unequal sides is called an irregular polygon. Among the alternatives given, only the triangle has unequal sides. The triangle is an irregular polygon.

11. D

Analyze each set of figures to determine what transformations have taken place.

The figure has been translated diagonally.

The figure has been translated to the right.

The figure has been flipped over a vertical flip line, making a mirror image.

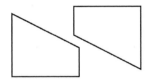

The figure has been turned or rotated 180°.

12. C

Since figure 2 is a mirror image of figure 1, the transformation that occurred was a reflection, or a flip, of figure 1 across the vertical line to create figure 2.

13. B

Alternative A is obtained by translating a square and an octagon vertically and horizontally.

Alternative C has spaces between the shapes, therefore it cannot be classified as a tiling pattern.

Alternative D is obtained by translating the shape vertically and horizontally.

The only way to obtain the inverted triangle in alternative B is to horizontally translate the upright triangle and then reflect it about a horizontal axis.

14. C

A translation slides a figure from one location to another without turning or changing the size or shape. The following design was created by translating the letter.

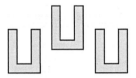

The only change is that the shape slides to different placements.

15. C

Step 1

Plot the coordinates.

When plotting points on a Cartesian plane, find the first coordinate on the *x*-axis. Then, move vertically upward until you find the second coordinate on the *y*-axis. Plot the point where the two axes intersect.

When the given points are plotted on the Cartesian plane, join them with straight lines.

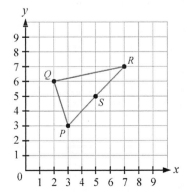

Step 2
Identify the shape made.
When the points are plotted and connected with straight lines, the shape formed is a triangle.

16. **D**

The first number in the coordinate (to the left of the comma) is the number located on the *x*-axis. The second number in the coordinate (to the right of the comma) is the corresponding number on the *y*-axis.

The design that Marcy drew will have a dot where each of the given coordinate pairs intersects on the grid.
(0, 1), (5, 2), (4, 5), and (1, 4).

This is the design that Marcy drew.

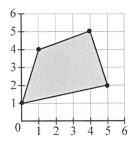

17. **D**

Step 1
Since the figure in position *A* is one square from the flip line, when it is flipped it must also be one square from the flip line. This would put the right angle coordinates at (6, 5).

Step 2
When the figure then slides one square to the right, the right angle coordinates become (7, 5).

Step 3
When the figure slides down two squares, the right angle coordinates are (7, 3), exactly where the right angle is shown on the graph for position *B*.

The transformation that flips the figure vertically, slides it right one, then slides it down two will move the figure from position *A* to *B*.

18. **D**

Step 1
Identify the transformation that occurred between the original image and image 1.
Image 1 is a mirror, or opposite, image of the original image.
The transformation that occurred between the original image and image 1 is a reflection.

Original   Image
shape   1

Step 2
Identify the transformation that occurred between image 1 and image 2.
Image 1 is turned to the right.
The transformation that occurred between image 1 and image 2 is a 90° clockwise rotation.

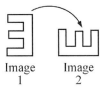

Image   Image
1   2

The series of transformations that occurred between the original image, image 1, and image 2 are a reflection and then a 90° clockwise rotation.

19. **WR**

Step 1
Perform the inverse transformation.
Trace the rotated image, and rotate in the opposite direction stated in the question.
The question said the rectangle moved counterclockwise. Rotate the traced image in the opposite direction, or clockwise.
Make sure the traced shape is directly on top of the image. Place the pencil on (5, 4). Turn the tracing paper 90°, or a $\frac{1}{4}$ turn to the right.

Step 2

Draw the rotated image on the Cartesian plane. Plot and label each new point to indicate that it is the original shape. Then, connect the points with line segments.

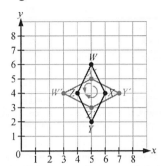

NOTES

Statistics and Probability

STATISTICS AND PROBABILITY

Table of Correlations

Outcome		Practice Questions	Unit Test Questions	Sample PAT Part A	Sample PAT Part B
6SP1.0	Collect, display and analyze data to solve problems.				
6SP1.1	*Create, label and interpret line graphs to draw conclusions.*	1, 2	1, 2	*Part A of the PAT tests Number outcomes across grades 4, 5, and 6.*	13
6SP1.2	*Select, justify and use appropriate methods of collecting data.*	3, 4	3, 4, 5		14
6SP1.3	*Graph collected data, and analyze the graph to solve problems.*	5, 6, 7	6, 7, 8, 9		15, 16
6SP2.0	Use experimental or theoretical probabilities to represent and solve problems involving uncertainty.				
6SP2.4	*Demonstrate an understanding of probability.*	8, 9, 10, 11	10, 11, 12, 13		26, 27, 40

6SP1.1 Create, label and interpret line graphs to draw conclusions.

LINE GRAPHS

A **line graph** uses points and lines to show how values change over a period of time.

If discrete data is plotted, the points are not connected with a line. **Discrete data** is data that has a limited number of values. For example, the months of the year, days of the week, or the number of students in a class. Discrete data is always presented as whole numbers. There are no values between the whole numbers.

A line graph plots continuous data as points and then joins the points with a line.
Continuous data is data that changes as time goes on. For example, weather patterns, temperatures, or a tree's height keep changing change over time.

Example

John bought 3 bottles of pop for $3.75. Stan bought 5 bottles of pop for $6.25. Chung bought 7 bottles of pop for $8.75.

Explain why the data presented is continuous or discrete.

Solution

Step 1
Identify the type of data presented.

The data presented is discrete data.

Step 2
Justify your answer.

Discrete data usually represents things that can be counted. The data is presented in the form of whole numbers with gaps between the numbers.

The data presented is discrete since there are no possible values between the whole numbers. For example, you cannot purchase a half bottle of pop or two and a quarter bottles of pop. You can only purchase pop by the bottle (whole number).

CREATING A LINE GRAPH

When creating a line graph, be sure you do the following:

- Label the axes.
- Add scales with intervals that suit the range and distribution of the data.
- Determine the coordinates for the ordered pairs.
- Plot the data correctly.
- Add a line segment connecting the continuous data.

Example

At a stationary store, a pen costs four times as much as a pencil. The following table shows the corresponding numbers of pens and pencils that can be purchased with the same amount of money.

Number of Pens	Number of Pencils
1	4
2	8
3	12
4	16
5	20

Draw a line graph to represent the information shown in the given table.

Solution

Step 1

Determine the coordinates from the ordered pairs.

The coordinates for this table of values are (1, 4), (2, 8), (3, 12), (4, 16), and (5, 20).

Step 2

Label the *x*-axis with the independent variable (number of pens) and the *y*-axis with the dependent variable (number of pencils). Choose an appropriate scale, and label the axes. Plot the coordinates on a graph. Since the data is discrete, do not join the dots that represent the coordinates.

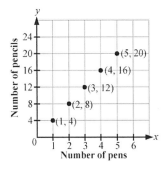

DRAWING CONCLUSIONS

Being able to read a line graph accurately and identify any existing patterns enables you to draw conclusions about the data. In order to draw conclusions, you need to consider all the information that you are given.

Example

This line graph shows the pay scale for hours worked per day at Chuck's Bike Shop.

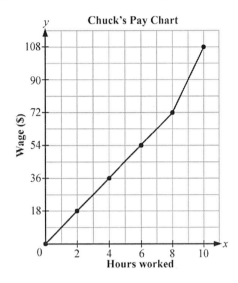

What conclusion can you draw about the wages employees can earn at Chuck's Bike Shop?

Solution

Step 1
Interpret the data shown.

- For every two hours worked up to eight hours, employees earn $18.
- For up to eight hours of work, employees earn $9 an hour.
- For two hours worked after eight hours, employees earn $36.
- For one hour worked after eight hours, employees earn $18.

Step 2
Draw a conclusion.

One conclusion you can draw is that working an eight-hour day is what most people do, since the pay stays the same for each hour. After eight hours, the wages per hour double.

Another conclusion you can draw is that Chuck's Bike Shop must really value the extra hours people work, since employees are paid double the normal wage for overtime hours.

Another conclusion you can draw is that the double wage will most likely continue if employees work more than 10 hours per day.

Use the following information to answer the next question.

When someone works longer than 8 h in a day, they are said to be working overtime. Donna uses the given graph to calculate overtime pay for her employees.

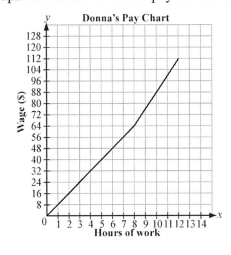

1. If Tammy works 12 h on Friday, how much should she be paid for that day's work?
   A. $64
   B. $96
   C. $112
   D. $128

Use the following information to answer the next question.

This graph shows the cost of a certain number of chocolate bars.

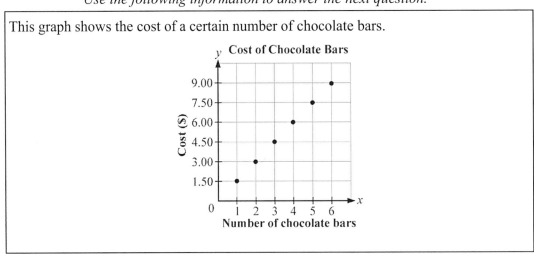

Written Response

2. If Mrs. Samuel bought $15 worth of chocolate bars, how many chocolate bars did she buy?

6SP1.2 Select, justify and use appropriate methods of collecting data.

SELECTING AND JUSTIFYING APPROPRIATE METHODS OF COLLECTING DATA

There are two types of data you can collect: primary data (sometimes called first hand data) and secondary data (sometimes called second hand data). When collecting **primary data**, you can use observations, perform experiments, conduct surveys, or design questionnaires. When collecting **secondary data**, you can read books and newspapers, access databases (information stored on a computer), or use electronic networks (Internet).

Choosing an appropriate method for collecting data depends on the type of question that you are trying to answer and the type of data you are trying to collect.

Example

Amanda keeps track of how many times she can toss a ball up in the air without dropping it.

Explain the method of data collection that Amanda is using.

Solution

If you collect data by doing an experiment, you carry out an action once or several times to gather results, which becomes the data. The action Amanda is carrying out is to toss the ball up into the air and then catch it. The results are the number of times she does not drop the ball. Amanda is performing an experiment to collect the data she wants. She is collecting primary data.

Example

One Tuesday, Colin counted the number of students who used the water fountain between 9:00 A.M. and 12:00 P.M.

Explain the method of data collection that Colin used.

Solution

Colin collected the data by observing the number of students that used the water fountain over the three-hour period. To collect data through observation, you watch something closely and record what is happening. Colin is collecting primary data.

Example

Amina asked the question, "What was the city of Edmonton's temperature high over the last 10 years on Canada Day?"

What method of data collection could Amina use to answer this question?

Solution

Amina cannot collect this data herself, so she will need to collect secondary data. Amina can look at a weather almanac on the Internet to determine the high temperature on Canada Day in Edmonton over the last 10 years.

Example

Tracy asked 25 classmates this question: "Which cereal do you prefer for breakfast: Choco Bites, Peanut Butter Delight, Rainbow Clusters, Cinnamon Squares, or something else?"

What method of data collection could Tracy use?

Solution

Tracy collected data by asking students to answer a given question. The students were given options to choose from. Tracy could use a written questionnaire where the students check off their choices, or she could ask students to raise their hands as she reads each option. Tracy could then record the number of students that choose each option. Tracy is collecting primary data.

Use the following information to answer the next question.

Gemma's aunt is an Olympic runner who is in training for the women's 1 500 m race. Gemma wants to collect information about the records set by the previous medal winners in this event for the last 10 Olympic Games.

3. To collect the **most reliable** information about the records set by the previous medal winners, Gemma should

   A. interview her aunt's coach

   B. visit a Museum of Ancient Olympic Games

   C. read a book about the Winter Olympic Games

   D. do research on the official website of the Olympic Games

4. Which of the following questions would require the collection of second-hand data?

   A. How long can you jump rope without stopping?

   B. How many hours of television do you watch each week?

   C. What is the favourite summer activity of Alberta's Grade 6 students?

   D. Should your Grade 6 class sell popcorn or cookies on Pyjama Day?

6SP1.3 Graph collected data, and analyze the graph to solve problems.

CREATING AND ANALYZING GRAPHS

Different forms of graphs can be used to represent the same data. However, one form is often more appropriate than another and allows the data to be presented more clearly and precisely.

Reading displayed data accurately enables you to draw conclusions, identify existing patterns, and formulate predictions about the data.

A **pictograph** is a graph that uses pictures or symbols to show and compare data.

Example

Mary-Ann and her class wanted to compare the number of earthworms in four different areas of soil around their school. They collected one bucket of soil from each area and sifted the soil through a screen so they could count the earthworms. Mary-Ann and her class found 20 worms in area *A*, 35 worms in area *B*, 25 worms in area *C*, and 30 worms in area *D*.

Draw a pictograph to represent the number of worms collected from each area. Make each drawn worm represent 10 actual worms.

Solution

Step 1

Figure out how many worms you need to draw for each area.

If 1 worm drawn equals 10 worms, there will need to be 2 worms drawn for area *A*,

$3\frac{1}{2}$ worms drawn for area *B*, $2\frac{1}{2}$ worms drawn for area *C*, and 3 worms drawn for area *D*.

Step 2

Draw the pictograph. Make sure to include a legend.

Area *A*	⌇⌇
Area *B*	⌇⌇⌇ˌ
Area *C*	⌇⌇ˌ
Area *D*	⌇⌇⌇

⌇ = 10 earthworms

A **bar graph** is a graph that displays facts about countable data using vertical or horizontal bars.

Example

This table shows how a certain group of junior high students spend their time in a typical day.

Activity	Hours per Day (h)
Sleeping	9.0
Eating	2.5
School	6.0
TV/Computer	3.0
Recreation	2.0
Other	1.5

Draw and label a graph to represent the information from the table.

Solution

Step 1

Make observations about the data.

The data is organized into categories: sleeping, eating, school, TV/computers, recreation, and other.

Step 2

Determine the graph, and justify your answer.

A bar graph is best used to display this data because the categories and the hours spent on each activity are given. The bar graph must include a title, a labelled horizontal axis, a labelled vertical axis, an appropriate scale, and bars to represent the data. Each category will be one bar, and the height of each bar will represent the hours spent on each activity.

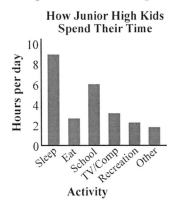

A **double bar graph** is a graph that is used to make comparisons between and within sets of data. A double bar graph uses two bars to compare separate pieces of information within the same category.

Example

Sabrina collected data about the favourite sports of students in the Grade 6 classes at her school. To display the data in a double bar graph, she first organized the information into two groups for each sport.

	Girls	Boys
Soccer	6	3
Volleyball	8	10
Baseball	5	7
Basketball	4	4

Draw and label a double bar graph to display the data Sabrina collected.

Solution

Step 1
Create the basic shell of the graph.

Label the *x*-axis and the *y*-axis, and use appropriate intervals for the axes. Add a title.

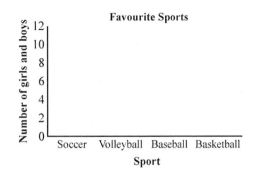

Step 2
Transfer the data from the table to the graph.

Make the two types of bars accurate and distinct, and join the bars for each specific sport. Create a legend for the data.

Place the numbers above the bars so you can easily see if you have drawn the bars accurately.

This double bar graph displays the data Sabrina collected.

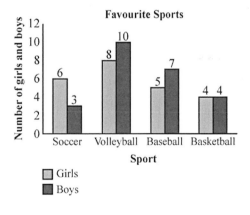

A **stem-and-leaf plot** organizes numerical data in increasing order. The purpose of a stem-and-leaf plot is to show the range and compare the frequency of data.

Example

Jonathan's class was practising for track and field. Jonathan kept a record of the number of meters each student ran.

Here is the list of Jonathan's results:
10, 25, 69, 28, 14, 67, 20, 20, 24, 30, 55, 15, 18, 57, 36, 38, 40, 45, 50, 68, 58, 60

Make a stem-and-leaf plot using the given information.

Solution

Step 1

Arrange the numbers in numerical order.
10, 14, 15, 18, 20, 20, 24, 25, 28, 30, 36, 38, 40, 45, 50, 55, 57, 58, 60, 67, 68, 69

Step 2

Separate the numbers into groups according to the digit in the tens position.

- 10, 14, 15, 18
- 20, 20, 24, 25, 28
- 30, 36, 38
- 40, 45
- 50, 55, 57, 58
- 60, 67, 68, 69

Step 3

Place the numbers in a stem-and-leaf plot.

Place the digit in the tens position on the left side of the vertical line. Place the corresponding ones digits on the right side of the line in ascending order.

This stem-and-leaf plot shows the given information.

Stem	Leaves
1	0, 4, 5, 8
2	0, 0, 4, 5, 8
3	0, 6, 8
4	0, 5
5	0, 5, 7, 8
6	0, 7, 8, 9

A **line graph** is a graph formed by a line that joins the points representing the data. A line graph is useful for showing changes over time.

Example

Kyle earns $7.50 per hour working at his uncle's landscaping company.

Use a graphical approach to show the total amount Kyle earns each hour during an 8-hour shift.

Solution

Step 1

Make observations about the data.

The data compares a unit of measure ($) over time.

Step 2

Determine the graph, and justify your answer.

A line graph will display the information best because it is an amount that Kyle is earning over a continuous time period (his 8-hour shift).

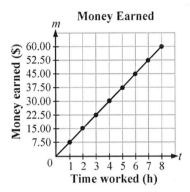

Although each type of graph has its own purpose, all graphs are used to organize and display data. Analyzing the data allows information to be understood more clearly. Data in graphs can also be used to solve problems.

Example

The number of azaleas and wildflowers in bloom over a four-week period in a particular garden are shown on this graph.

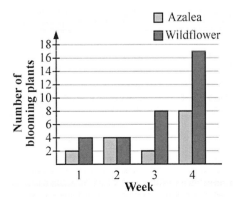

Determine how many more wildflowers than azaleas bloomed in total during the four-week period.

Solution

Step 1

Determine the number of azaleas that bloomed during the four-week period.

Read the bars for the number of azaleas blooming each week. Then, determine the sum for all four weeks.

$2 + 4 + 2 + 8 = 16$

Step 2

Determine the number of wildflowers that bloomed during the four-week period.

Read the bars for the number of wildflowers blooming each week. Then, determine the sum for all four weeks.

$4 + 4 + 8 + 17 = 33$

Step 3

Subtract the two sums to calculate the difference.

$33 - 16 = 17$

In total, there were 17 more wildflowers than azaleas blooming during the given period.

Use the following information to answer the next question.

The data in the table shows the preferences of Grade 7 students in Springfield Junior High regarding the activities they enjoy doing during their leisure time.

Activity	Number of Students
Dancing	25
Painting	20
Reading	15
Sports	30
Music	25

5. The data in the table would **best** be represented by a

A. bar graph

B. frequency table

C. broken line graph

D. stem-and-leaf plot

Use the following information to answer the next question.

The given stem and leaf plot shows student scores for a particular test.

Stem	Leaves
3	4, 5, 5, 6
4	0, 0, 2, 9
5	0, 0

Numerical Response

6. How many students received a score? _____

Use the following information to answer the next question.

Trisha surveys students in her class by asking them each a question. She makes this graph to show the results of the survey.

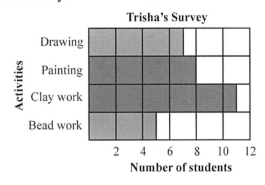

7. To get the results shown on the graph, which of the following survey questions could Trisha have asked the students?

   A. Is your favourite subject art?

   B. Do you prefer to paint or draw?

   C. Do you want to be a part of my survey?

   D. Which art class activity do you like the most?

6SP2.4   Demonstrate an understanding of probability.

PROBABILITY

An **outcome** is a possible result of an event. **Probability** is the likelihood that a particular outcome will occur. In a probability experiment you determine all the possible outcomes of a particular event.

Example

Shabir wanted to know all the possible outcomes of tossing two coins at the same time.

Create a chart to help him determine the number of possible outcomes.

Solution

Step 1

Create a table with three headings.

Outcome	Coin 1	Coin 2

Step 2

Complete the table with all the possible combinations of heads and tails.

Outcome	Coin 1	Coin 2
1	Heads	Heads
2	Tails	Tails
3	Heads	Tails
4	Tails	Heads

There are four possible outcomes when tossing two coins.

Theoretical probability is the chance of an outcome occurring under ideal circumstances. It can also be expressed as a decimal number between 0 and 1.

Example

What is the theoretical probability of rolling a 3 on a six-sided die?

Solution

Step 1

Determine the number of favourable outcomes.

The favourable outcome is rolling a 3, so there is 1 favourable outcome.

Step 2

Determine the total possible outcomes.

The possible outcomes for rolling the die are 1, 2, 3, 4, 5, and 6. There are 6 possible outcomes.

Step 3

Calculate the probability of the desired event.

Substitute the values into the probability formula.

$$P_{\text{(favourable outcome)}} = \frac{\text{number of favourable outcomes}}{\text{total possible outcomes}}$$

$$P_{(3)} = \frac{1}{6}$$

The theoretical probability of rolling a 3 on a six-sided die is $\frac{1}{6}$.

Experimental probability is dependent on the results of an experiment. It is calculated by dividing the number of times an outcome occurs by the number of times the event was tested.

As the number of trials in an experiment increases, the experimental probability will get closer to the theoretical probability.

Example

Sam rolls a standard six-sided number cube 60 times. The following chart shows the number of times the cube landed on each of the six numbers.

Number on Cube	Number of Times
1	12
2	5
3	13
4	10
5	17
6	3

In Sam's trial, which number on the cube had the same theoretical probability as experimental probability?

Solution

Step 1

Determine the theoretical probability.

Since there are six different numbers on the cube, the theoretical probability of landing on any one of the numbers is $\frac{1}{6}$.

Step 2

Determine the experimental probability.

For the experimental probability to be the same as the theoretical probability, the experimental probability fraction must be equivalent to $\frac{1}{6}$.

Since the denominator of the experimental probability will be 60 (total number of rolls), the numerator must be 10 (the number of times the cube landed on a particular number).

$$\frac{1}{6} = \frac{10}{60}$$

Step 3

Determine which number had the same theoretical and experimental probabilities.

The cube landed 10 times on the number 4. This is shown by the probability $\frac{10}{60} = \frac{1}{6}$.

The number 4 has the same theoretical probability as experimental probability.

Use the following information to answer the next question.

Farmer Macgavin's hens laid 50 eggs. Of the 50 eggs, 35 were white, and 15 were brown.

8. When he gathered the eggs, what is the probability that the first egg he randomly picked was a white egg?

   A. $\frac{1}{50}$ B. $\frac{1}{35}$

   C. $\frac{3}{7}$ D. $\frac{7}{10}$

Use the following information to answer the next question.

Matthew is target shooting with his bow and arrow. Out of 4 attempts, he hits the target once.

9. Based on the experimental probability, if Matthew attempts to hit his target 100 times, how many times might he hit the target?

   A. 40   B. 35

   C. 25   D. 20

Use the following information to answer the next question.

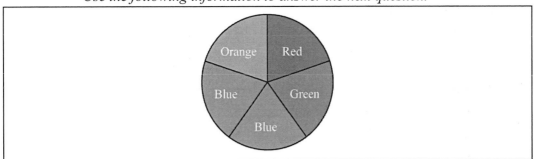

10. What is the theoretical probability of spinning blue on the given spinner?

A. $\dfrac{1}{5}$ 　　　　　　　　B. $\dfrac{2}{5}$

C. $\dfrac{3}{5}$ 　　　　　　　　D. $\dfrac{4}{5}$

Use the following information to answer the next question.

A spinner is shown.

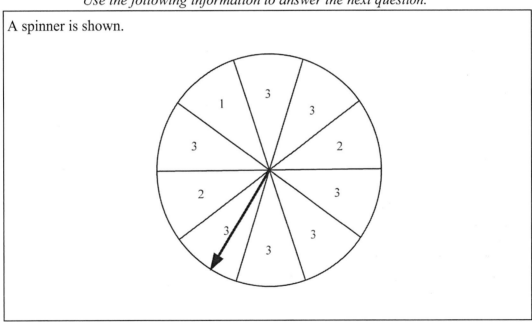

11. What is the probability of the given spinner stopping on the number 3?

A. $\dfrac{10}{3}$ 　　　　　　　　B. $\dfrac{10}{7}$

C. $\dfrac{7}{10}$ 　　　　　　　　D. $\dfrac{3}{10}$

ANSWERS AND SOLUTIONS
STATISTICS AND PROBABILITY

1. C	4. C	7. D	10. B
2. WR	5. A	8. D	11. C
3. D	6. 10	9. C	

1. C

To determine how much money Tammy made working for 12 h, find 12 along the horizontal x-axis. Follow the vertical grid line up to where it meets the line of the graph. Next, follow the horizontal grid line toward the y-axis of the graph. The value found on the vertical axis is the amount of money Tammy earns after working for 12 h.

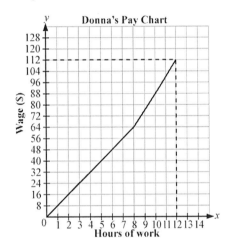

Tammy will be paid $112 for 12 h of work.

2. WR

Step 1

Examine how the cost changes for each additional bar.

- 1 bar costs $1.50.
- 2 bars cost $3.00. $1.50 + $1.50 = $3.00
- 3 bars cost $4.50. $3.00 + $1.50 = $4.50
- 4 bars cost $6.00. $4.50 + $1.50 = $6.00

The pattern rule is to add $1.50 for each additional bar.

Step 2

Apply the pattern rule by starting with $9.00 (the greatest cost shown on the graph) and adding $1.50 until you get to $15.00. Every time you add $1.50, increase the number of chocolate bars by 1.

- For $9.00, you get 6 bars (shown on graph).
- For $10.50, you get 7 bars.
  $9.00 + $1.50 = $10.50
- For $12.00, you get 8 bars.
  $10.50 + $1.50 = $12.00
- For $13.50, you get 9 bars.
  $12.00 + $1.50 = $13.50
- For $15.00, you get 10 bars.
  $13.50 + $1.50 = $15.00

Mrs. Samuel bought 10 chocolate bars with $15.00.

3. D

Step 1

Examine each option to determine the kind of information Gemma will collect.

- If Gemma interviews her aunt's coach, she will collect a lot of information about the records her aunt has set. The coach may be able to recount certain memorable medal winners from previous years, but she would most likely need to use other sources to help Gemma with the kind of data she wants to collect.
- The focus of a Museum of Ancient Olympic Games is on the early history of the Olympics. Gemma would not learn anything about recent performances in the 1 500 m race over the last 10 Olympic games, since the last forty years is not considered ancient. However, she may learn a lot about the history of racing.
- Since running races are only part of the Summer Olympic Games, reading a book about the Winter Olympic Games would not give Gemma the information she wants.
- An official website of the Olympic Games would most likely give Gemma the most complete and updated information about all the Olympic sports and medal winners.

Step 2

Match the method of collecting information with the kind of information Gemma wants.

Since Gemma wants information about the records set by medal winners in a particular race over the last 10 years, she would most likely get the most accurate and recent information by researching the official website of the Olympic Games.

4. C

Second-hand data would need to be collected to discover the favourite summer activity of Alberta's Grade 6 students. To find the most popular activity for students across the whole province, the surveyor would rely on other sources of information rather than just questioning the students. It would be an almost impossible task to ask every student in the province.

5. A

A bar graph is used to compare two or more values corresponding to some items in a given set.

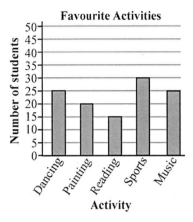

A broken line graph shows how the same set of data changes over time.

The data is already in a frequency table.

A stem-and-leaf plot is used to organize a large set of data, and since the data set is small, the stem-and-leaf plot is not useful here.

6. 10

Step 1

Match the stem with each leaf to determine the scores achieved.

- 34, 35, 35, 36
- 40, 40, 42, 49
- 50, 50

Step 2

Count the number of scores.
$4 + 4 + 2 = 10$

According to the stem and leaf, 10 students received a score.

7. D

To find what question Trisha asked, look at the information given on the graph.

The graph lists four different art activities. It also gives a number of students for each activity.

That means that the question had to be about art activities. The numbers could refer to how many students chose each activity.

The survey question that Trisha could have asked is "Which art class activity do you like the most?"

8. D

Step 1

Determine the number of favourable outcomes. The favourable outcome is a white egg. There are 35 favourable outcomes.

Step 2

Determine the total possible outcomes. There are a total of 50 eggs and therefore 50 possible outcomes.

Step 3

Calculate the probability of the desired event. Substitute the values into the probability formula.

P(favourable outcome)

$$= \frac{\text{number of favourable outcomes}}{\text{total possible outcomes}}$$

$$P(\text{white}) = \frac{35}{50}$$
$$= \frac{35 \div 5}{50 \div 5}$$
$$= \frac{7}{10}$$

9. C

Step 1

Determine the experimental probability.

$$\frac{\text{Occurred}}{\text{Tested}}$$

Matthew only hit the target once out of four attempts, so the experimental probability for Matthew's four attempts is $\frac{1}{4}$.

Step 2

Make a prediction based on the theoretical probability.

Based on the actual results, you can predict the results of 100 attempts by making an equivalent fraction to $\frac{1}{4}$.

Think of a number that the denominator 4 can be multiplied by to make a hundred. You can multiply 4 by 25 to make a hundred. You also need to multiply the numerator 1 by the same number, 25.

$$\frac{1}{4} = \frac{25}{100}$$

Out of 100 attempts, the experimental probability could be $\frac{25}{100}$, which means that Matthew might hit the target 25 times out of 100 attempts.

10. B

Step 1

Determine the number of favourable outcomes. The favourable outcome is blue. There are 2 favourable outcomes.

Step 2

Determine the total possible outcomes. The possible outcomes for spinning the spinner are blue, blue, green, red, and orange. There are 5 possible outcomes.

Step 3

Calculate the probability of the desired event. Substitute the values into the probability formula.

$$P_{\text{favourable outcome}} = \frac{\text{number of favourable outcomes}}{\text{total possible outcomes}}$$

$$P_{\text{blue}} = \frac{2}{5}$$

11. C

The spinner has 10 parts, so the denominator of the probability fraction is 10.

Of the 10 parts, seven parts are labelled with the number 3, so the numerator of the probability fraction is 7.

The probability that the spinner will stop on the number 3 is $\frac{7}{10}$.

Copyright Protected

UNIT TEST — STATISTICS AND PROBABILITY

Use the following information to answer the next question.

At a pizza restaurant, the owner increases the cost of a medium pizza whenever there is an increase in the cost of cheese. The given table shows the cost of cheese, measured in dollars per pound, that corresponds to the cost of a medium pizza.

Cost of Cheese ($ per pound)	Cost of Medium Pizza ($)
3	$4
4	$6
5	$8
6	$10
7	$12

1. Which of the following graphs represents the information in the given table?

A.

B.

C.

D.

Unit Test

164

Castle Rock Research

Use the following information to answer the next question.

> On the same day, Kim planted one bean seed in Pot A and another bean seed in Pot B. She then placed Pot A on a windowsill and Pot B on the kitchen table. She recorded the heights of the two plants at the end of each week. The given graph plots the growth of each plant for seven weeks.

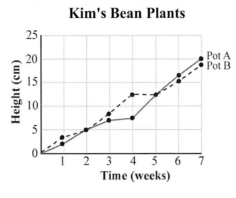

2. The bean plants in Pot A and Pot B were the same height at the end of weeks

    A. 1 and 6   **B.** 2 and 5

    C. 5 and 6   **D.** 5 and 7

Use the following information to answer the next question.

> Marco wanted to buy a popular action figure for his collection. He checked with four different sources to find the price of the action figure.
>
> - Marco went to one store and saw that the action figure had a price tag of $10.
> - He saw a store flier for another store that listed the price of the figure as $8.
> - His friend Jesse told him that yesterday's newspaper advertised the same figure for $12.
> - Marco saw a television commercial advertising that the figure would be on sale on Saturday for $6.

3. The source that provides first hand data is the price that Marco

    A. read in the flier   **B.** saw in the store

    C. saw on television   **D.** read in the newspaper advertisement

Use the following information to answer the next question.

For a school project, Nicole wants to find out how many hours a day the students in her Grade 6 class spend watching television. She also wants to know how many hours they spend studying.

4. In order to collect this data **most effectively**, Nicole would probably choose to
   A. design and conduct an experiment
   B. design and use a structured questionnaire
   C. make observations and chart the information
   D. use electronic networks, such as the Internet

Use the following information to answer the next question.

Karen goes to a small school where there is only one class for each grade level from kindergarten to Grade 6. On Valentine's Day, she decides to find out how many students in her school are wearing red shirts or sweaters.

5. Which of the following methods is **most appropriate** to collect this data?
   A. Conducting a survey   B. Performing an experiment
   C. Using personal observation   D. Selecting data from a database

Use the following information to answer the next question.

The data in the table shows the average daily temperature in a city over the course of a week.

Day of the Week	Temperature (°C)
Monday	26
Tuesday	36
Wednesday	32
Thursday	34
Friday	36
Saturday	24
Sunday	28

6. The data in the given table is **best** represented using a
   A. bar graph   B. circle graph
   C. broken-line graph   D. stem-and-leaf plot

Use the following information to answer the next question.

Price of Gas ($)	
January	0.89
February	0.94
March	0.97
April	1.00
May	1.10
June	1.14
July	1.15
August	1.13
September	1.08
October	1.04
November	0.99
December	0.97

7. Which type of graph would **best** display the information in the given table?

   A. Bar graph   **B.** Line graph

   C. Pictograph   **D.** Circle graph

Use the following information to answer the next question.

DVD Sales by Genre	
Genre	**Sales (%)**
Horror	15
Comedy	25
Romance	25
Children's movies	20
Suspense	15

8. Which of the following types of graphs would **best** display the information in the given table?

   A. Bar graph   **B.** Line graph

   C. Pictograph   **D.** Circle graph

Anna and her friend Karina both love shoes.

- Anna has 18 different coloured pairs of flip flops, 11 pairs of boots, 12 pairs of high heels, and 9 different kinds of sneakers.
- Karina has 20 different coloured pairs of flip flops, 9 pairs of boots, 9 pairs of high heels, and 11 different kinds of sneakers.

Written Response

9. Explain the type of graph that would be **most appropriate** to use to record the kinds of shoes that Anna and Karina own.

Use the following information to answer the next question.

The spinner shown is divided into 10 equal sections.

10. If Eileen spins the spinner once, what is the probability that the spinner will land on a number that has a 2 in it?

A. $\dfrac{1}{2}$ B. $\dfrac{3}{5}$

C. $\dfrac{7}{10}$ D. $\dfrac{4}{5}$

11. Jackie has a bag containing 2 red marbles, 4 green marbles, and 6 blue marbles. Jackie did an experiment and found that she chose a red marble 4 out of 10 times. Which of the following tables shows the results of Jackie's experiment?

A.
Experimental Probability	Theoretical Probability
0.40	$\frac{1}{6}$

B.
Experimental Probability	Theoretical Probability
0.12	$\frac{1}{12}$

C.
Experimental Probability	Theoretical Probability
0.04	$\frac{2}{5}$

D.
Experimental Probability	Theoretical Probability
0.02	$\frac{5}{12}$

Use the following information to answer the next question.

Two six-sided dice are rolled at the same time. The sum of the two numbers is 9.

12. Which of the following sets of numbers represents all the possible outcomes of rolling a sum of 9?

A. (4, 5), (3, 6)

B. (4, 5), (3, 6), (2, 7)

C. (4, 5), (5, 4), (3, 6), (6, 3)

D. (4, 5), (3, 6), (3, 3), (5, 4)

13. When Natalie tosses a twelve-sided number cube five times and finds that the number six comes up four times, she is demonstrating

A. an experimental probability

B. a theoretical probability

C. an impossible event

D. a certain event

Copyright Protected

ANSWERS AND SOLUTIONS — UNIT TEST

1. A	5. C	9. WR	13. A
2. B	6. C	10. C	
3. B	7. B	11. A	
4. B	8. D	12. C	

1. A

Step 1

Write a set of ordered pairs.

Create ordered pairs with the independent value (cost of cheese) first and the dependent value (cost of medium pizza) second.

Cost of Cheese	Cost of Medium Pizza	Ordered Pair
3	4	(3, 4)
4	6	(4, 6)
5	8	(5, 8)
6	10	(6, 10)
7	12	(7, 12)

Step 2

Draw and label a grid with the x-axis and the y-axis, using appropriate increments and a title.

The independent variable is cost of cheese, so it is placed along the x-axis. The dependent variable is the cost of the medium pizza, so it is placed along the y-axis.

Step 3

Plot the ordered pairs on the graph.

For each ordered pair, start at the origin, move along the x-axis to find the value of the x-coordinate, then, move up vertically to the value of the y-coordinate.

The graph in alternative A is correct.

2. B

Step 1

Compare the heights of the plants at the end of each week.

If the dot on the straight line that represents the height of the plant in Pot A and the dot on the dotted line that represents the height of the plant in Pot B have a space between them, the plants are not the same height.

- In weeks 1, 3, and 4, the plant in Pot A is shorter than the plant in Pot B.
- In weeks 6 and 7, the plant in Pot A is taller than the plant in Pot B.

Step 2

If the two lines meet and the dot is shared, the coordinates for the heights of both plants will be the same. This means that the two plants are the same height.

- In week 2, Pot A and Pot B have the same coordinates of (2, 5). The two lines share the same dot.
- In week 5, Pot A and Pot B have the same coordinates of (5, 12). The two lines share the same dot.

The bean plants in Pot A and Pot B were the same height at the end of weeks 2 and 5.

3. B

Firsthand data is information that you collect on your own. It is information that is collected directly. Second hand data is not collected directly by the researcher, but is obtained from another source.

The price that Marco actually saw in the store is an example of firsthand data.

The prices that Marco read in the flier, saw on the television advertisement, and heard about in the newspaper advertisement are examples of secondhand data.

4. B

Nicole wants to find out how many hours a day students in her Grade 6 class spend watching television and how many hours they spend studying. In order to gather data for her project, she must decide which method of collecting the information will best suit her needs. The best way for Nicole to gather the information she needs would be for her to design and use a structured questionnaire. In this way, she would be able to gather the personal data from each of her classmates that she requires.

Designing an experiment to collect this data would not be appropriate because an experiment could not provide the information Nicole needs. It would also be very difficult to gather this information through observation. The time spent watching television and studying is personal to each student and is not information that would be found on the Internet.

5. C

Observation is the best way to collect data when it is possible to count things that can be seen, such as the number of red shirts or sweaters the students are wearing. Since the school is small, Karen can easily observe each class by herself (with the teachers' permission) and count the number of students wearing red shirts or sweaters.

Karen could also appoint one student from each class to observe and record the number of red shirts worn in that class. Then, Karen could collect these numbers in order to determine a total count.

6. C

A broken-line graph is used to show the change in a quantity over time. Since the data illustrates how the average temperature is changing on a daily basis, the data is best represented by using a broken-line graph.

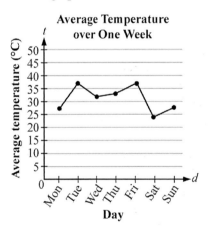

7. B

A line graph plots continuous data as points and then joins them with a line. The data collected is usually measured against time, which allows you to observe the change that occurs in the data over a period of time.

Copyright Protected

8. D

Step 1

Make observations about the data.

The sales of the DVDs are given as percentages. That means that the parts, the different genres, are being compared to the whole, their total sales as a group.

Step 2

Determine the best graph to use, and justify your answer.

Circle graphs are best for illustrating the relationship between parts of a whole.

Since the sales of different genres of DVDs are being compared to their sales as a whole in percentages, a circle graph best displays the data.

9. WR

Step 1

Determine the most appropriate type of graph.

The most appropriate type of graph to use is a double bar graph.

Step 2

Justify your answer.

A double bar graph is best to show two sets of similar data, making it easy to compare the data. In this question, the similar data is the four kinds of shoes that the two girls own (flip flops, boots, high heels, and sneakers). One set of data is the number of each kind of shoes Anna owns.

The other set of data is the number of kinds of shoes Karina owns. Each set of side-by-side bars will show a comparison of each particular kind of shoe that both Anna and Karina own.

10. C

Step 1

Determine the number of favourable outcomes.

- The favourable outcome is a number with a 2 in it.
- The numbers 72, 2, 32, 22, 20, 12, and 27 have the digit 2 in them.
- There are 7 favourable outcomes.

Step 2

Determine the total possible outcomes.

The possible outcomes for spinning the spinner are 17, 27, 77, 72, 2, 32, 18, 22, 20, and 12. There are 10 possible outcomes.

Step 3

Calculate the probability of the desired event. Substitute the values into the probability formula.

$$P_{outcome} = \frac{\text{number of favourable outcomes}}{\text{total possible outcomes}}$$

$$P_{\# \text{ with a } 2} = \frac{7}{10}$$

11. A

To calculate the experimental probability as shown in the table, convert the probability from ratio form to decimal form:

$$4:10 \rightarrow \frac{4}{10} = 4 \div 10 = 0.40$$

To calculate the theoretical probability, use the probability formula:

$$P(\text{red}) = \frac{\text{number of red marbles}}{\text{total number of marbles}}$$

$$P(\text{red}) = \frac{2}{12} = \frac{1}{6}$$

12. C

Step 1

Determine which numbers will result in a sum of 9.

One combination of numbers that will result in a sum of 9 is 4 and 5.

Another combination of numbers that will result in a sum of 9 is 3 and 6.

Step 2

Determine the total number of possible combinations.

1. You can roll a 4 on the first die and a 5 on the second die.
2. You can roll a 5 on the first die and a 4 on the second die.
3. You can roll a 3 on the first die and a 6 on the second die.
4. You can roll a 6 on the first die and a 3 on the second die.

The set of numbers that represents all the possible combinations is (4, 5), (5, 4), (3, 6), (6, 3).

13. A

Natalie is conducting an experiment to obtain the given results, which is an example of an experimental probability.

Theoretical probability is a mathematical calculation of the probability that an event will occur in an ideal situation.

An impossible event will *never* occur and has a probability of 0.

A certain event will *always* happen and has a probability of 1.

NOTES

Success on Tests

KEY STRATEGIES FOR SUCCESS ON TESTS

AN OVERVIEW OF THE TEST

This section is all about the skills and strategies you need to be successful on the Alberta Mathematics 6 Provincial Achievement Test. It is designed for you to use together with your classroom learning and assignments.

FINDING OUT ABOUT THE TEST

Here are some questions you may wish to discuss with your teacher to help you prepare for the Alberta Mathematics 6 Provincial Achievement Test.

1.	What will this test assess or cover?	The test will assess your ability to understand and apply the mathematical concepts you have learned throughout the year. The test is divided into two parts: Part A and Part B. Part A will assess your foundational skills in Number. Part B will assess the expectations from 4 Mathematics Content Strands: (Number, Patterns and Relations, Shape and Space, and Statistics and Probability).
2.	What materials can I bring to write the **Part A** of the test?	You need to bring a pencil and an eraser. You may also choose to bring manipulatives such as a ruler, tracing paper, pattern blocks, tiles and cubes, geoboards, tangrams, counters, spinners, and number lines. **Multiplication Tables and Calculators are not allowed.**
3.	What materials can I bring to write the **Part B** of the test?	You need a pencil, an eraser, and a calculator. You may also choose to bring manipulatives such as a ruler, tracing paper, pattern blocks, tiles and cubes, geoboards, tangrams, counters, spinners, and number lines. **Multiplication Tables and Scientific or Graphing Calculators are not allowed.**
4.	Are there any materials provided for the test?	No Any formulas that students need for answering Grade 6 Mathematics questions are provided.
5.	What is the format of the test?	**Part A** has 15 numerical-response questions that are worth one point each. **Part B** has 40 multiple-choice questions that are worth one point each
6.	How much time do I have to write the test?	**Part A** is designed to be completed in 20 minutes but students may take a total of 40 minutes. **Part B** is designed to be completed in 70 minutes but students may take a total of 140 minutes.
7.	How important is this test to my final grade?	Your teacher can answer this question.

Having a good understanding of effective test taking skills can help you do well on the test. Being familiar with the question format may help you in preparing for quizzes, unit tests, or year-end tests.

This section is all about the skills and strategies you need to be successful on tests. It is designed for you to use together with your classroom learning and assignments.

THINGS TO CONSIDER WHEN TAKING A TEST

It is normal to feel anxious before you write a test. You can manage this anxiety by using the following strategies:

- Think positive thoughts. Imagine yourself doing well on the test.
- Make a conscious effort to relax by taking several slow, deep, controlled breaths. Concentrate on the air going in and out of your body.
- Before you begin the test, ask questions if you are unsure of anything.
- Jot down key words or phrases from any instructions your teacher gives you.
- Look over the entire test to find out the number and kinds of questions on the test.
- Read each question closely and reread if necessary.
- Pay close attention to key vocabulary words. Sometimes these are **bolded** or *italicized*, and they are usually important words in the question.
- If you are putting your answers on an answer sheet, mark your answers carefully. Always print clearly. If you wish to change an answer, erase the mark completely and then ensure your final answer is darker than the one you have erased.
- Use highlighting to note directions, key words, and vocabulary that you find confusing or that are important to answering the question.
- Double-check to make sure you have answered everything before handing in your test.

When taking tests, students often overlook the easy words. Failure to pay close attention to these words can result in an incorrect answer. One way to avoid this is to be aware of these words and to underline, circle, or highlight them while you are taking the test.

Even though some words are easy to understand, they can change the meaning of the entire question, so it is important that you pay attention to them. Here are some examples.

all	always	most likely	probably	best	not
difference	usually	except	most	unlikely	likely

Example

1. Which of the following equations is **not** correct?

    A. $3 + 2 = 5$

    B. $4 - 3 = 1$

    C. $5 \times 4 = 15$

    D. $6 \times 3 = 18$

HELPFUL STRATEGIES FOR ANSWERING MULTIPLE-CHOICE QUESTIONS

A multiple-choice question gives you some information, and then asks you to select an answer from four choices. Each question has one correct answer. The other answers are distractors, which are incorrect. Below are some strategies to help you when answering multiple-choice questions.

- Quickly skim through the entire test. Find out how many questions there are and plan your time accordingly.

- Read and reread questions carefully. Underline key words and try to think of an answer before looking at the choices.

- If there is a graphic, look at the graphic, read the question, and go back to the graphic. Then, you may want to underline the important information from the question.

- Carefully read the choices. Read the question first and then each answer that goes with it.

- When choosing an answer, try to eliminate those choices that are clearly wrong or do not make sense.

- Some questions may ask you to select the best answer. These questions will always include words like best, most appropriate, or most likely. All of the answers will be correct to some degree, but one of the choices will be better than the others in some way. Carefully read all four choices before choosing the answer you think is the best.

- If you do not know the answer, or if the question does not make sense to you, it is better to guess than to leave it blank.

- Do not spend too much time on any one question. Make a mark (*) beside a difficult question and come back to it later. If you are leaving a question to come back to later, make sure you also leave the space on the answer sheet, if you are using one.

- Remember to go back to the difficult questions at the end of the test; sometimes clues are given throughout the test that will provide you with answers.

- Note any negative words like no or not and be sure your choice fits the question.

- Before changing an answer, be sure you have a very good reason to do so.

- Do not look for patterns on your answer sheet, if you are using one.

Helpful Strategies for Answering Numerical-Response Questions

The new Part A test consists of 15 numerical-response questions, so this type of question is now very important to understand.

The Part A numerical-response questions are designed to test your ability calculate the answer to a particular addition, subtraction, multiplication, or division problem. The numerical-response questions on the Part A test will require you to do these calculations without the use of a calculator.

Responses to numerical-response questions are recorded in an answer sheet. Keep the following tips in mind as you fill in the answer sheet:

- Fill in the boxes above the bubble answers from left to right.
- Not every answer will need all four boxes filled in. In fact, you may only need to fill one box to complete the answer.
- You may need to fill a decimal point into the second or third box.
- If your answer includes a decimal less than one, include a zero in the first box before the decimal point.
- Fill in the circle below the answer box that matches the answer you placed in the box. For example, if you entered a zero in the first box, fill in the circle containing a zero below the answer box.
- To help you manage your time, you can choose to leave the bubbles blank as you write the answer in the boxes. Then, once you have answered each question, you can fill in the bubbles quickly as you review your answers.

ABOUT MATHEMATICS TESTS

WHAT YOU NEED TO KNOW ABOUT MATHEMATICS TESTS

To do well on a mathematics test, you need to understand and apply your knowledge of mathematical concepts. Reading skills can also make a difference in how well you perform. Reading skills can help you follow instructions and find key words, as well as read graphs, diagrams, and tables. They can also help you solve mathematics problems.

Mathematics tests usually have two types of questions: questions that ask for understanding of mathematics ideas and questions that test how well you can solve mathematics problems.

HOW YOU CAN PREPARE FOR THE MATHEMATICS TEST

Below are some strategies that are particular to preparing for and writing mathematics tests.

- Know how to use your calculator and, if it is allowed, use your own for the test.
- Note-taking is a good way to review and study important information from your class notes and textbook.
- Sketch a picture of the problem, procedure, or term. Drawing is helpful for learning and remembering concepts.
- Check your answer to practice questions by working backward to the beginning. You can find the beginning by going step-by-step in reverse order.
- When answering questions with graphics (pictures, diagrams, tables, or graphs), read the test question carefully.
    - o Read the title of the graphic and any key words.
    - o Read the test question carefully to figure out what information you need to find in the graphic.
    - o Go back to the graphic to find the information you need.
- Decide which operation is needed.
- Always pay close attention when pressing the keys on your calculator. Repeat the procedure a second time to be sure you pressed the correct keys.

TEST PREPARATION COUNTDOWN

If you develop a plan for studying and test preparation, you will perform well on tests.

Here is a general plan to follow seven days before you write a test.

Countdown: 7 Days before the Test

1. Use "Finding Out About the Test" to help you make your own personal test preparation plan.

2. Review the following information:
   - areas to be included on the test
   - types of test items
   - general and specific test tips

3. Start preparing for the test at least 7 days before the test. Develop your test preparation plan and set time aside to prepare and study.

Countdown: 6, 5, 4, 3, 2 Days before the Test

1. Review old homework assignments, quizzes, and tests.

2. Rework problems on quizzes and tests to make sure you still know how to solve them.

3. Correct any errors made on quizzes and tests.

4. Review key concepts, processes, formulas, and vocabulary.

5. Create practice test questions for yourself and then answer them. Work out many sample problems.

Countdown: The Night before the Test

1. The night before the test is for final preparation, which includes reviewing and gathering material needed for the test before going to bed.

2. Most important is getting a good night's rest and knowing you have done everything possible to do well on the test.

Test Day

1. Eat a healthy and nutritious breakfast.

2. Ensure you have all the necessary materials.

3. Think positive thoughts: "I can do this." "I am ready." "I know I can do well."

4. Arrive at your school early so you are not rushing, which can cause you anxiety and stress.

SUMMARY OF HOW TO BE SUCCESSFUL DURING A TEST

You may find some of the following strategies useful for writing a test:

- Take two or three deep breaths to help you relax.
- Read the directions carefully and underline, circle, or highlight any important words.
- Look over the entire test to understand what you will need to do.
- Budget your time.
- Begin with an easy question, or a question you know you can answer correctly, rather than following the numerical question order of the test.
- If you cannot remember how to answer a question, try repeating the deep breathing and physical relaxation activities first. Then, move on to visualization and positive self-talk to get yourself going.
- When answering a question with graphics (pictures, diagrams, tables, or graphs), look at the question carefully.
  - Read the title of the graphic and any key words.
  - Read the test question carefully to figure out what information you need to find in the graphic.
  - Go back to the graphic to find the information you need.
- Write down anything you remember about the subject on the reverse side of your test paper. This activity sometimes helps to remind you that you do know something and you are capable of writing the test.
- Look over your test when you have finished and double-check your answers to be sure you did not forget anything.

Practice Tests

SAMPLE PROVINCIAL ACHIEVEMENT TEST PART A

AN OVERVIEW OF THE TEST

Part A of the Alberta Mathematics 6 Provincial Achievement Test (PAT) has 15 numerical-response questions that are worth one point each. The test is designed to test a student's foundational skills in the Number content strand.

The following Table of Correlations indicates how each of the items on the Sample PAT Part A test is aligned to Alberta curriculum outcomes.

Table of Correlations			
Grade		Outcome	Sample PAT Part A
4	*N.3*	*Demonstrate an understanding of addition of numbers with answers to 10 000 and their corresponding subtractions (limited to 3- and 4-digit numerals) by using personal strategies for adding and subtracting, estimating sums and differences, and solving problems involving addition and subtraction.*	2, 7
5	*N.5*	*Demonstrate, with and without concrete materials, an understanding of multiplication (2-digit by 2-digit) to solve problems.*	4, 10
5	*N.6*	*Demonstrate, with and without concrete materials, an understanding of division (3-digit by 1-digit), and interpret remainders to solve problems.*	5
5	*N.11*	*Demonstrate an understanding of addition and subtraction of decimals (limited to thousandths).*	1, 3, 6, 8, 9
6	*N.8*	*Demonstrate an understanding of multiplication and division of decimals.*	12, 13, 14, 15
6	*P.5*	*Demonstrate and explain the meaning of preservation of equality, concretely and pictorially.*	11

PART A ANSWER SHEET

You can find a sample Answer Sheet in the Appendices section on **page 217** of this book to practise filling in the numerical-response answer sheets. This sheet may be cut or torn out of the book to be used in conjunction with the Part A tests. Practising the act of filling in the numerical response answer fields will help prepare the student for answering questions in an unfamiliar format.

For further assistance in completing the numerical-response questions on the Sample PAT Part A Test, please see the strategies for answering numerical-response questions in the "Key Strategies for Success on Tests" section of this book.

SAMPLE PROVINCIAL ACHIEVEMENT TEST PART A
(NO CALCULATOR)

1. What is 26.3 – 11.2?

   Answer: _____

2. What is 4 678 + 2 331?

   Answer: _____

3. What is 36.6 + 23.3?

   Answer: _____

4. What is 29 × 13?

   Answer: _____

5. What is 555 ÷ 5?

   Answer: _____

6. What is 5 + 0.4 + 7.82?

   Answer: _____

7. What is 4 876 – 3 241?

   Answer: _____

8. What is 7.7 – 3.25?

   Answer: _____

9. What is 4 – 1.23?

   Answer: _____

10. What is 34 × 21?

    Answer: _____

Use the following information to answer the next question.

$56.7 - 3\_.9 = 17.8$

11. In the equation above, which digit could be put in place of the blank to make the equation correct?

    Answer: _____

12. What is 37.6×5?

    Answer: _____

13. What is $48.6 \div 2$?

    Answer: _____

14. What is $6.36 \div 6$?

    Answer: _____

15. What is $56.94 \div 6$?

    Answer: _____

SAMPLE PROVINCIAL ACHIEVEMENT TEST PART B

Use the following information to answer the next question.

The given pattern of stars has five rows.

Row 1 ☆☆☆☆☆☆☆☆☆☆☆☆☆☆☆☆

Row 2 ☆☆☆☆☆☆☆☆☆☆☆☆☆☆

Row 3 ☆☆☆☆☆☆☆☆☆☆☆☆

Row 4 ☆☆☆☆☆☆☆☆☆☆

Row 5 ☆☆☆☆☆☆☆☆

1. The pattern of stars translated into a numeric pattern would be

   A. 8, 10, 12, 14, 16   **B.** 8, 10, 12, 16, 18

   C. 16, 14, 12, 10, 8   **D.** 18, 16, 12, 10, 8

Use the following information to answer the next question.

Sarah decided to solve 5 math questions each night for one week, beginning on Monday.

2. Which of the following graphs correctly shows the total number of math questions Sarah answered by the end of Thursday night?

   A.

   B.

   C.
   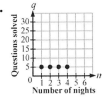

   D.
   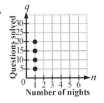

Use the following information to answer the next question.

Mia uses this chart to help her determine how many grams of beef and beans she needs to make chili.

Number of servings	Grams of beef	Grams of beans
4	500	175
6	750	350
8	1 000	525
10	1 250	700
12	1 500	875

3. For every 2 servings, how many more grams of beef and beans does Mia need?

   A. 500 g more of beef and 175 g more of beans

   B. 250 g more of beef and 150 g more of beans

   C. 250 g more of beef and 175 g more of beans

   D. 150 g more of beef and 175 g more of beans

Use the following information to answer the next question.

Miss Bandar gave Rob the pattern of numbers in the given chart. She asked him to complete the pattern and then represent the completed pattern using numbered tiles.

| 3 | 6 | 9 | 12 | ? | ? | ? | ? |

Rob arranged the numbered tiles in a square to show the completed pattern of numbers from the chart.

He started at the top left corner of the square. He placed a blank tile after each numbered tile.

4. Which of the following squares represents the completed pattern of numbers from the chart?

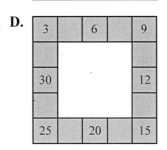

Use the following information to answer the next question.

A number pattern is shown.

42, ?, 28, 21, 14

5. If $x = 42$, then which of the following expressions can be used to find the missing number in the given pattern of numbers?

A. $x + (28 - 21)$ B. $x - (28 - 21)$

C. $x \div (28 - 21)$ D. $x - (28 \div 21)$

Use the following information to answer the next question.

A food store displays a basket containing 59 pieces of fruit. Of those 59 pieces of fruit, 15 are apples, 20 are oranges, and the rest are bananas.

6. Which of the following equations correctly represents the number of bananas, z?
   A. $z = 59 + 20 + 15$ **B.** $z = 59 - 20 + 15$
   C. $z = 59 - 15 + 20$ **D.** $z = 59 - (15 + 20)$

Use the following information to answer the next question.

Problem: The difference between two numbers is 10 000. One of the numbers is 4 895. What is the other number?

7. In each of the following equations, the unknown is represented by a variable. Which of the following equations **cannot** be used to solve the given problem?
   A. $10\ 000 - 4\ 895 = N$ **B.** $10\ 000 - R = 4\ 895$
   C. $Q = 4\ 895 + 10\ 000$ **D.** $4\ 895 + Z = 10\ 000$

Use the following information to answer the next question.

Mr. Cahill has a problem. He bought 1 000 bricks for a total cost of $120.00, and now he is wondering how much he paid for each individual brick.

8. Which of the following equations **cannot** be used to solve Mr. Cahill's problem?
   A. $1\ 000 \div \$120 = \nabla$ **B.** $\$120 \times \nabla = 1\ 000$
   C. $1\ 000 \div \nabla = \$120$ **D.** $\$120 \times 1\ 000 = \nabla$

Use the following information to answer the next question.

A rectangular garden has a length of 14 feet (ft) and a width of 11 ft. Molly wants to divide the garden into equal-sized sections so she can plant 7 different kinds of vegetables. She writes an equation to find the size of each section using g to represent the area of each section.

9. Which of the following equations could Molly use to find the area of each section of the garden?
   A. $14 \times 11 - 7 = g$ **B.** $14 \times 11 \div 7 = g$
   C. $14 + 11 + 7 = g$ **D.** $14 \times 11 \times 7 = g$

10. To preserve equality in the equation $5 \times 12 \times k = 960 \div 8$, the value of k must be
    A. 120   **B.** 60
    C. 6   **D.** 2

Marnie started with the 0° mark on the right side of the protractor to measure angle *AOB*.

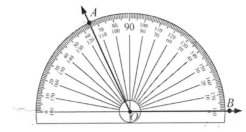

11. What is the measure of the angle shown in this diagram?

A. 125°	**B.** 115°
C. 75°	**D.** 65°

Use the following information to answer the next question.

The dimensions of a right rectangular prism are given in inches (in):

- The length is 7 in.
- The width is 5 in.
- The height is 2 in.

12. What will happen to the volume of the right rectangular prism if the length is doubled?

A. The new volume will be half the original volume.

B. The new volume will be twice the original volume.

C. The new volume will be 7 times the original volume.

D. The new volume will be 14 times the original volume.

Use the following information to answer the next question.

Joseph Christian "Jaws" Chestnut is a competitive eater who won the 92nd Annual Nathan's Hot Dog Eating Contest. The linear relation 5.5x, where x is the number of minutes, can be used to represent the number of hotdogs he consumed.

13. Which of the following graphs represents the number of hotdogs "Jaws" ate over the course of the competition?

A.
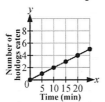

B.
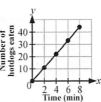

C.
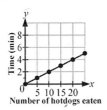

D.
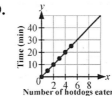

Use the following information to answer the next question.

Stella plants a bean plant as part of a project for science class. At the end of the project, Stella must hand in a report stating how much the plant grew over a period of five weeks.

14. Which of the following methods of data collection would **most** help Stella collect the information she needs?

A. Survey   **B.** Experiment

C. Observation   **D.** Measurement

Use the following information to answer the next question.

Students at Midtown School were surveyed to see how they get to school. The results are shown in the given graph.

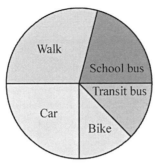

May, Melody, Deborah, and Amy each wrote two conclusions based on the data in the graph. They then indicated if their conclusions were true or false.

Amy	More than half of the students walk or take the school bus.	False
	The number of students riding in cars is the same as the number of students biking and taking the transit bus together.	True
Deborah	There are more students taking the transit bus than the school bus.	False
	The number of students riding in cars is the same as the number of students biking and taking the transit bus together.	False
May	The number of students riding in cars is the same as the number of students riding the school bus.	True
	The number of students riding in cars is the same as the number of students biking and taking the transit bus together.	False
Melody	Half of the students walk or take the school bus.	False
	There are more students taking the transit bus than the school bus.	True

15. Which of the students correctly indicated if their conclusions were true or false?
   A. Amy
   B. Deborah
   C. May
   D. Melody

16. For an assignment, a class wants to show the number of people who wear glasses by age group. The type of graph the class would **most likely** choose to effectively show the comparison is a
   A. circle graph
   B. pictograph
   C. line graph
   D. bar graph

17. If each of the three angles of a triangle measures 60°, the triangle is called
   A. a right triangle
   B. a scalene triangle
   C. an obtuse triangle
   D. an equilateral triangle

18. Which of the following figures is a regular polygon?

A.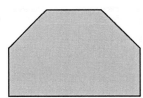

B.

C.

D.

Use the following information to answer the next question.

Triangle 1 was rotated clockwise about point *A* to form Triangle 2, as shown in the diagram.

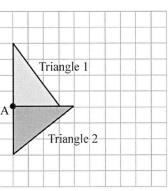

19. How many degrees was the triangle rotated?

A. 0°

B. 90°

C. 180°

D. 270°

20. Which of the following designs is **not** an example of a translation?

A.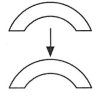

B.

C.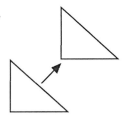

D.

Use the following information to answer the next question.

Josie plotted these points on a coordinate grid.

- Point *A*: (2, 2)
- Point *B*: (3, 3)
- Point *C*: (2, 5)
- Point *D*: (0, 3)

She then joined the points in this order: *A → B → C → D → A*

21. Which of the following designs did Josie make?

A.

B.

C.

D.

Use the following information to answer the next question.

Luis plots point *P* on a coordinate plane at the location (4, 3). He increases the *x*-coordinate by 3 and increases the *y*-coordinate by 1 in order to plot point *Q*.

22. What are the coordinates of point *Q*?

A. (1, 2)   B. (3, 1)

C. (5, 6)   D. (7, 4)

Use the following information to answer the next question.

Shawn uses the coordinates (1, 3), (3, 3), and (1, 5) to plot the vertices of a triangle on a grid.

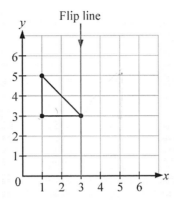

He then flips the triangle over the flip line and slides it down two spaces.

23. After the two transformations, the coordinates for the vertices of the triangle will be

A. (3, 1), (5, 3), (3, 3)   **B.** (3, 1), (5, 1), (5, 3)

C. (5, 1), (3, 1), (3, 3)   **D.** (5, 3), (7, 3), (7, 5)

Use the following information to answer the next question.

A shape is drawn on a grid.

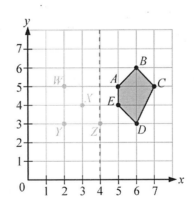

24. What is the new position of point *D* after a reflection across the mirror line?

A. Point *W*   **B.** Point *X*

C. Point *Y*   **D.** Point *Z*

Use the following information to answer the next question.

The given grid shows a rectangle tiled with square units.

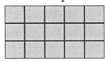

25. Which of the following expressions can be used to find the area of the given rectangle?

A. $5 + 3$ **B.** 5×3

C. $5 + 3 + 5 + 3$ **D.** $5 \times 3 \times 5 \times 3$

Use the following information to answer the next question.

Carlton has three pencils of different colours: red, yellow, and black. He also has two sharpeners of different colours: white and green.

26. If Carlton used one pencil and one pencil sharpener at a time, how many possible combinations can he make?

A. 5   **B.** 6

C. 7   **D.** 8

Use the following information to answer the next question.

Joel earns $150 per week mowing lawns in his neighborhood. He charges a $5 gas fee for each lawn that he mows and a service fee of $25 per lawn.

27. Which equation represents the number of lawns (n) Joel mows per week?

A. $150 = 25 + 5n$ **B.** $150 = 25n + 5$

C. $150 = n(25 + 5)$ **D.** $150 = 25(n + 5)$

28. The number 178.009 can be read as

A. one hundred seventy-eight and nine

B. one hundred seventy-eight decimal nine

C. one hundred seventy-eight and nine hundredths

D. one hundred seventy-eight and nine thousandths

Use the following information to answer the next question.

Jennifer purchased a balloon bouquet of seven balloons for her mother's birthday. The masses of the individual balloons are 5.75 g, 4.15 g, 4.756 g, 5.25 g, 3.893 g, 4.58 g, and 4.184 g. All of the balloons are tied to a weight with a mass of 25 g.

29. What is the mass of the entire balloon bouquet, including the weight?

    A. 57.56 g   **B.** 57.563 g

    C. 575.63 g   **D.** 575.6 g

Use the following information to answer the next question.

When a group of students walked into their classroom, the math problem $9\ 635 + 3\ 099 + 897 = ?$ was written on the board. Each of the students estimated the sum. The given chart shows the estimates made by four of the students.

Name	Estimate
Emily	13 500
Sarah	13 000
Marcus	12 500
Donald	14 000

30. Which student's estimate is closest to the actual sum?

    A. Emily   **B.** Sarah

    C. Marcus   **D.** Donald

31. In which of the following tables are the numbers classified correctly?

A.

Number	7	27
Classification	Prime	Prime

B.

Number	9	19
Classification	Composite	Prime

C.

Number	3	23
Classification	Prime	Composite

D.

Number	2	22
Classification	Composite	Composite

32. Expressed as an improper fraction, the mixed number $13\frac{1}{2}$ is

A. $\frac{14}{2}$　　　　　　　　　B. $\frac{16}{2}$

C. $\frac{26}{2}$　　　　　　　　　D. $\frac{27}{2}$

33. Which of the following sets of mixed numbers and improper fractions have equivalent values?

A. $3\frac{3}{4}$ and $\frac{15}{4}$　　　　　　　　　B. $3\frac{1}{4}$ and $\frac{10}{4}$

C. $2\frac{3}{4}$ and $\frac{8}{4}$　　　　　　　　　D. $1\frac{1}{4}$ and $\frac{7}{4}$

Use the following information to answer the next question.

Rose and Ashley each have 15 candies.

34. If Ashley gave 3 of her candies to Rose, then the ratio of Ashley's candies to the total number of candies is

A. 1:3　　　　　　　　　B. 2:3

C. 2:5　　　　　　　　　D. 3:5

35. In the month of July, it was sunny on 15 days, rainy on 12 days, and overcast on 4 days. What is the ratio of sunny days to rainy days?

A. 1 to 6　　　　　　　　　B. 4 to 5

C. 5 to 4　　　　　　　　　D. 15 to 2

Use the following information to answer the next question.

Max has a length of rope that is 100 m long. He cuts off a piece that is 25% of the total length.

36. The length of the piece of rope that Max has left is

A. 25 m　　　　　　　　　B. 50 m

C. 75 m　　　　　　　　　D. 100 m

37. Which of the following number lines represents the correct order of the integers −12, 8, 5, and −2?

A.

C.

B.

D.

38. Which of the following lists presents the fractions in descending order?

   A. $\dfrac{7}{2}, \dfrac{10}{6}, \dfrac{13}{8}, \dfrac{4}{3}$ **B.** $\dfrac{4}{3}, \dfrac{13}{8}, \dfrac{10}{6}, \dfrac{7}{2}$

   C. $\dfrac{10}{6}, \dfrac{4}{3}, \dfrac{13}{8}, \dfrac{7}{2}$ **D.** $\dfrac{13}{8}, \dfrac{7}{2}, \dfrac{10}{6}, \dfrac{4}{3}$

Use the following information to answer the next question.

The total mass of 8 doughnuts is 655.2 g.

39. What is the mass of each individual doughnut?

   A. 8.19 g   **B.** 80.7 g

   C. 81.9 g   **D.** 647.2 g

Use the following information to answer the next question.

A spinner is divided into six equal parts. Two parts of the spinner are red, two parts are green, and two parts are blue, as shown in the diagram. The spinner is spun 30 times, and it stops on red 12 times.

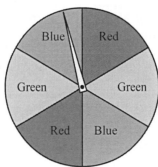

40. When the experimental probability of the spinner stopping on red is compared to the theoretical probability, the experimental probability is

   A. the same as the theoretical probability

   B. less than the theoretical probability by 2

   C. less than the theoretical probability by $\dfrac{1}{15}$

   D. greater than the theoretical probability by $\dfrac{1}{15}$

ANSWERS AND SOLUTIONS — SAMPLE PROVINCIAL ACHIEVEMENT TEST PART A (NO CALCULATOR)

1. 15.1	5. 111	9. 2.77	13. 24.3
2. 7009	6. 13.22	10. 714	14. 1.06
3. 59.9	7. 1635	11. 8	15. 9.49
4. 377	8. 4.45	12. 188	

1. 15.1

Step 1

Write the question vertically. Align the decimal points.

$$\begin{array}{r} 2\,6\,.\,3 \\ -1\,1\,.\,2 \\ \hline \end{array}$$

Step 2

Subtract. Regroup when necessary.

$$\begin{array}{r} {}^{1\ 16}\!\!\!\!\cancel{2\,6}\,.\,3 \\ -1\,1\,.\,2 \\ \hline 1\,5\,.\,1 \end{array}$$

The value of 26.3 – 11.2 is 15.1.

2. 7009

Step 1

Write the question vertically.

$$\begin{array}{r} 4\ 678 \\ +2\ 331 \\ \hline \end{array}$$

Step 2

Add. Regroup when necessary.

$$\begin{array}{r} {}^{1\ 1} \\ 4678 \\ +2\ 331 \\ \hline 7\ 009 \end{array}$$

$4\ 678 + 2\ 331 = 7\ 009$

3. 59.9

Step 1

Write the question vertically. Align the decimal points.

$$\begin{array}{r} 36.6 \\ +23.3 \\ \hline \end{array}$$

Step 2

Add. Regroup when necessary.

$$\begin{array}{r} 36.6 \\ +23.3 \\ \hline 59.9 \end{array}$$

$36.6 + 23.3 = 59.9$

4. 377

Step 1

Write the question vertically.

$$\begin{array}{r} 29 \\ \times\ 13 \\ \hline \end{array}$$

Step 2

Multiply. Regroup when necessary.

$$\begin{array}{r} {}^{2} \\ 29 \\ \times\ 13 \\ \hline {}^{1} \\ 87 \\ +290 \\ \hline 377 \end{array}$$

$29 \times 13 = 377$

5. 111

Step 1

Write the question vertically.

$$5\overline{)555}$$

Step 2

Divide. Regroup when necessary.

$$\begin{array}{r} 111 \\ 5\overline{)555} \\ \underline{-5} \\ 5 \\ \underline{-5} \\ 5 \\ \underline{-5} \\ 0 \end{array}$$

$555 \div 5 = 111$

6. 13.22

Step 1

Write the question vertically. Align the decimal points. Put zeros as placeholders to make addition easier.

```
  5.00
  0.40
+7.82
```

Step 2

Add. Regroup when necessary.

```
   1
  5.0
  0.40
+7.82
 13.22
```

$5 + 0.4 + 7.82 = 13.22$

7. 1635

Step 1

Write the question vertically.

```
  4 876
− 3 241
```

Step 2

Subtract. Regroup when necessary.

```
  4 876
− 3 241
  1 635
```

$4\ 876 - 3\ 241 = 1\ 635$

8. 4.45

Step 1

Write the question vertically. Align the decimal points. Put zeros as placeholders to make the subtraction easier.

```
  7.70
−3.25
```

Step 2

Subtract. Regroup when necessary.

```
    6 17
  7.70
−3.25
  4.45
```

$7.7 - 3.25 = 4.45$

9. 2.77

Step 1

Write the question vertically. Align the decimal points. Put zeros as placeholders to make the subtraction easier.

```
  4.00
−1.23
```

Step 2

Subtract. Regroup when necessary.

```
  3 9 10
  4.00
−1.23
  2.77
```

$4 - 1.23 = 2.77$

10. 714

Step 1

Write the question vertically.

```
   34
× 21
```

Step 2

Multiply. Regroup when necessary.

```
   34
× 21
   1
   34
+680
  714
```

$34 × 21 = 714$

11. 8

Step 1

To determine the number with the blank space, write the question as $56.7 − 17.8$.

Step 2

Write the question vertically. Align the decimal points.

```
  56.7
−17.8
```

Step 3

Subtract. Regroup when necessary.

$$\begin{array}{r} {}^{4}\!\!\!\not5\,{}^{15}\!\!\!\not6\,.\,{}^{17}\!\!\!\not7 \\ -1\,7\,.\,8 \\ \hline 3\,8\,.\,9 \end{array}$$

$56.7 - 17.8 = 3\underline{8}.9$

The missing digit in the equation
$56.7 - 3\_.9 = 17.8$ is the digit 8.

12. 188

Step 1

Write the question vertically.

$$\begin{array}{r} 37.6 \\ \times\quad 5 \end{array}$$

Step 2

Multiply. Regroup when necessary.

$$\begin{array}{r} {}^{33} \\ 37.6 \\ \times\quad 5 \\ \hline 188.0 \end{array}$$

$37.6 \times 5 = 188$

13. 24.3

Step 1

Write the question vertically. Align the decimal point in the quotient with the decimal point in the divisor.

$2\overline{)48.6}$

Step 2

Divide. Regroup when necessary.

$$\begin{array}{r} 24.3 \\ 2\overline{)48.6} \\ \underline{-4} \\ 8 \\ \underline{-8} \\ 6 \\ \underline{-6} \\ 0 \end{array}$$

$48.6 \div 2 = 24.3$

14. 1.06

Step 1

Write the question vertically. Align the decimal point in the quotient with the decimal point in the divisor.

$6\overline{)6.36}$

Step 2

Divide. Regroup when necessary.

$$\begin{array}{r} 1.06 \\ 6\overline{)6.36} \\ \underline{-6} \\ 3 \\ \underline{-0} \\ 36 \\ \underline{-36} \\ 0 \end{array}$$

$6.36 \div 6 = 1.06$

15. 9.49

Step 1

Write the question vertically. Align the decimal point in the quotient with the decimal point in the divisor.

$6\overline{)56.94}$

Step 2

Divide. Regroup when necessary.

$$\begin{array}{r} 9.49 \\ 6\overline{)56.94} \\ \underline{-54} \\ 29 \\ \underline{-24} \\ 54 \\ \underline{-54} \\ 0 \end{array}$$

$56.94 \div 6 = 9.49$

ANSWERS AND SOLUTIONS — SAMPLE PROVINCIAL ACHIEVEMENT TEST PART B

1. C	9. B	17. D	25. B	33. A
2. B	10. D	18. B	26. B	34. C
3. C	11. B	19. B	27. C	35. C
4. C	12. B	20. D	28. D	36. C
5. B	13. B	21. C	29. B	37. A
6. D	14. D	22. D	30. A	38. A
7. C	15. A	23. B	31. B	39. C
8. D	16. D	24. C	32. D	40. D

1. C

Step 1

Count the number of stars in each row.

- Row 1 has 16 stars.
- Row 2 has 14 stars.
- Row 3 has 12 stars.
- Row 4 has 10 stars.
- Row 5 has 8 stars.

Step 2

Determine the numeric pattern.

Record the numbers of stars in the same order as the rows, placing commas between the numbers.

The given visual pattern can be translated into the numeric pattern 16, 14, 12, 10, 8.

2. B

Step 1

Label the x-axis and the y-axis.

The x-axis represents the number of nights and increases by 1.

The y-axis represents the questions solved and increases by 5.

Step 2

Plot points on the graph.

On the first night, Sarah answered 5 questions. This point has the coordinates $(1, 5)$.

On the second night, Sarah answered 5 more questions. She has now answered 10 questions in total. This point has the coordinates $(2, 10)$.

On the third night, Sarah answered 5 more questions and has answered a total of 15 questions. This point has the coordinates $(3, 15)$.

On Thursday, the fourth night, Sarah answered 5 more questions. She has now answered a total of 20 questions. This is the point $(4, 20)$.

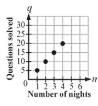

3. C

Step 1

The pattern shows that the amount of beef increases. Find the difference between each amount:

$1\ 500 - 1\ 250 = 250$
$1\ 250 - 1\ 000 = 250$
$1\ 000 - 750 = 250$
$750 - 500 = 250$

Therefore, the amount of beef increases by 250 g for every two servings.

Step 2

The pattern shows that the amount of beans increases. Find the difference between each amount:

$875 - 700 = 175$
$700 - 525 = 175$
$525 - 350 = 175$
$350 - 175 = 175$

Therefore, each amount of beans increases by 175 g for every two servings.

Mia needs 250 g more of beef and 175 g more of beans for every two servings.

4. C

This square represents the completed pattern of numbers from the chart:

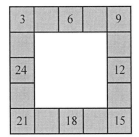

The pattern rule for the numbers in the chart is "add 3 each time."

3	6	9	12	15	18	21	24

5. B

Step 1

First, you need to determine the pattern rule being used. To do this, you need to examine the numbers to see how they change from term to term.

One way to do this is to find the difference between 28 and 21 and between 21 and 14.

$28 - 21 = 7$
$21 - 14 = 7$

The pattern rule is to subtract 7 from each term to get the next term.

Step 2

Since $x = 42$, you need to subtract 7 from 42 or 7 from x to determine the missing number. The expression $42 - 7$ has the same value as $x - 7$.

The value of 7 can also be expressed as $(28 - 21)$ or $(21 - 14)$.

The expression that can be used to determine the missing number is $x - (28 - 21)$.

6. D

Step 1

Determine what is known and what is not known.

The total amount of fruit (59 pieces) and two parts (15 apples and 20 oranges) of the total three are known. The third part, the number of bananas, is represented by the variable z.

Fruit $= 59$
Apples $= 15$
Oranges $= 20$
Bananas $= z$

Step 2

Create an equation to solve for z.

Add the two known parts and subtract that sum from the total amount of fruit. This gives the unknown part represented by z.

$z = 59 - (15 + 20)$

7. C

The equation $Q = 4\ 895 + 10\ 000$ **cannot** be used to solve the given problem.

In this equation, the letter Q does not represent the other number.

In the other three equations, the variable represents the missing number, regardless of what letter is used for the variable.

8. D

The symbol ∇ represents the unknown number, which is the cost of a single brick.

To determine the equations that can be used to solve the problem, you can divide the number of bricks bought by the total cost, or you can divide the number of bricks bought by the unknown number (the cost of a single brick).

$1\ 000 \div \$120 = \nabla$
$1\ 000 \div \nabla = \$120$

Since multiplication is the inverse operation of division, these equations can also be used to solve the problem.
$\$120 \times \nabla = 1\ 000$
$\nabla \times \$120 = 1\ 000$

The equation that cannot be used to solve the given problem is $\$120 \times 1\ 000 = \nabla$.
You cannot determine the cost of a single brick by multiplying the total cost of the bricks by the number of bricks. In this equation, the symbol ∇ does not represent the cost of a single brick.

9. B

Step 1
Multiply the length and the width of the garden to find its area.
14×11

Step 2
Divide the total area by 7 to find the area of each section.
$14 \times 11 \div 7 = g$
The equation that Molly could use to find the area of each section of the garden is
$14 \times 11 \div 7 = g$.

10. D

Step 1
Perform the operation on the side that does not have a variable.
In this case, the right side does not have a variable.
$960 \div 8 = 120$
Since the right side of the equation is equal to 120, the left side of the equation must also be equal to 120.

Step 2
Multiply the two whole numbers on the left side of the equation.
$5 \times 12 = 60$
You now know that $60 \times k = 120$.
In order to preserve equality, you need to perform the same operation on both sides of the equation. You can do this by dividing both sides by 60.
$60 \div 60 \times k = 120 \div 60$
$k = 2$

Step 3
Check your work.
Substitute the number 2 for the variable k.
$5 \times 12 \times k = 960 \div 8$
$60 \times 2 = 120$
$120 = 120$
To preserve equality in the equation
$5 \times 12 \times k = 960 \div 8$, the value of k must be 2.

11. B

Step 1
Start on the right side of the protractor at the $0°$ mark on the inner scale, and count up to the number nearest to ray AO,
but not crossing the ray.
10, 20, 30, ...90, 100, 110

Step 2
Count the ticks by ones from 110 to where ray AO crosses the scale.
...111, 112, 113, 114, 115
The measure of the other angle shown in the diagram is $115°$.

12. B

Method 1
Calculate the volume of the prism before and after the change, then compare.

Step 1
Determine the volume of the prism.
$V = lwh$
$V = 7 \times 5 \times 2$
$V = 70$

Step 2
Determine the new volume of the prism after the length is doubled.
$V = lwh$
$V = 14 \times 5 \times 2$
$V = 140$
When the length is doubled, the new volume will be two times the original volume.

Method 2
Think about how the formula will change.

Step 1
Write the formula for the prism before the change.
$V = lwh$
$V = 7 \times 5 \times 2$

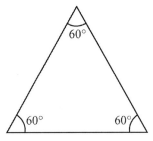

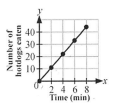

Step 2

Write the formula for the prism after the change.

$V = lwh$

$V = (2 \times 7) \times 5 \times 2$

Change the grouping of the numbers being multiplied.

$V = (2 \times 7) \times 5 \times 2$

$V = 2 \times (7 \times 5 \times 2)$

The volume of the new prism is two times the volume of the original prism.

13. B

Using the relation $5.5x$, create a table of values to determine the coordinates of the points.

Time (min)	Hotdogs
0	0
1	5.5
2	11
3	16.5
4	22
5	27.5
6	33
7	38.5
8	44

When the points $(0, 0)$, $(2, 11)$, $(4, 22)$, $(6, 33)$, $(8, 44)$ are plotted, the following graph is obtained:

14. D

The best method of data collection for Stella's purpose is measurement. Measurement is best used when recording changes over time. Since Stella is recording changes in the height of the bean plant, she will use measurements obtain her data.

A survey is the best way to collect data when you want to find out the opinions of a group of people. An experiment is the best way to collect data when determining the probability of an event. Observation is the best way to collect data when you want to count things you can see.

15. A

Amy is the student who correctly indicated that her conclusions were true or false. A circle graph represents information as parts of a whole. Usually, the amounts in each sector are represented in percentages so that all amounts total 100%. The inferences that were made from the circle graph were correct. Half of the students walk or take the school bus. One fourth of the students riding bikes and taking the transit bus is equivalent to one fourth of the students riding cars.

16. D

Bar graphs are used to compare data in different categories and to describe the relationship of several variables all at once. In this case, the total number of people wearing eyeglasses is the data being considered. The categories are the various age groups.

17. D

An angle measuring 60° is also known as an acute angle because it is less than 90°.

An acute triangle contains three acute angles.

A special kind of acute triangle is an equilateral triangle because it has three equal side lengths as well as three equal angle measures.

A triangle with each of its three angles measuring 60° is called an equilateral triangle.

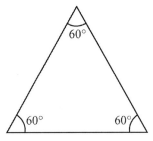

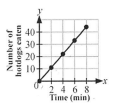

18. B

All the sides of a regular polygon are equal in length, and all the angles of a regular polygon are identical. There is only one polygon that fits this description.

19. B

The triangle was rotated clockwise 90°.

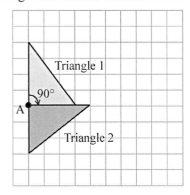

20. D

The following design is not an example of a translation because the figure has flipped to create an opposite image.

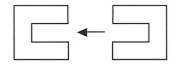

A translation, or slide, is the movement of a figure in which each point of the figure is moved the same distance and direction. Only the location of the figure changes in a translation.

21. C

The first number in the coordinate is the number located on the *x*-axis.

The second number in the coordinate is the corresponding number on the *y*-axis.

The design that Josie drew will have a dot where each of the given coordinate pairs intersect on the grid.

(2, 2), (3, 3), (2, 5), (0, 3)

This is the design that Josie drew.

22. D

In an ordered pair representing a point on a grid, the first number represents the *x*-coordinate and the second number represents the *y*-coordinate.

To find the location of point Q, increase each coordinate of point P by the amount given.

Step 1
Add 3 to the *x*-coordinate.
$4 + 3 = 7$

Step 2
Add 1 to the *y*-coordinate.
$3 + 1 = 4$

The coordinates of point Q are (7, 4).

23. B

Step 1
Flip the triangle across the flip line.
See how the coordinates change:

• The coordinates of vertex (3, 3) will still be (3, 3).
• The coordinates of vertex (1, 3) will now be (5, 3).
• The coordinates of vertex (1, 5) will now be (5, 5).

After the flip, the coordinates of the triangle will be (3, 3), (5, 3), and (5, 5).

Step 2
Slide the triangle down 2 units.
See how the coordinates change:

• The coordinates of vertex (3, 3) will now be (3, 1).
• The coordinates of vertex (5, 3) will now be (5, 1).
• The coordinates of vertex (5, 5) will now be (5, 3).

After the slide (the second transformation), the coordinates will be (3, 1), (5, 1), and (5, 3).

24. C

A reflection is a figure that has been flipped over a mirror line. The flipped image will be the same size but will be reversed.

Both the original image and the flipped image must be the same distance from the mirror line. Each vertex will be the same distance from the mirror line.

In the original image, point D is 2 units away from the mirror line. In the reflected image, point Y is also 2 units away from the mirror line.

Point Y is the new position of point D.

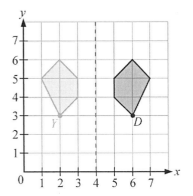

25. B

Step 1

Calculate the area using addition.
Count the number of squares in each row.
There are 5 squares in each row.
Since there are 3 rows, add 5 three times.
$5 + 5 + 5 = 15$

Step 2

Calculate the area using multiplication.
Count the number of squares in each row.
There are 5 squares in each row.
Since there are 3 rows, multiply 5 by 3.
$5 \times 3 = 15$

Step 3

Select the correct expression.
Of the four given expressions, the only one that can be used to find the area of the rectangle is 5×3.

26. B

One way to determine all the possible outcomes (combinations) is to make a tree diagram. Match the white sharpener with each colour of pencil. Then match the green sharpener with each colour of pencil.

Sharpeners	Pencils	Outcomes
White	Red	White - Red
	Yellow	White - Yellow
	Black	White - Black
Green	Red	Green - Red
	Yellow	Green - Yellow
	Black	Green - Black

Another way to determine the total number of combinations is to multiply the number of sharpeners (2) by the number of different coloured pencils (3).
$2 \times 3 = 6$

Using one pencil and one sharpener at a time, Carlton can make 6 different combinations.

27. C

Step 1

Write an equation using words instead of numbers.
The amount that Joel earns is equal to the service fee multiplied by the number of lawns mowed plus the gas fee multiplied by the number of lawns mowed.

Step 2

Substitute numbers or variables into the word equation: $150 = (5 \times n) + (25 \times n)$, which is the same as $150 = n(25 + 5)$.
The equation that represents the number of lawns Joel mows is $150 = n(25 + 5)$.

28. D

Step 1

Read the whole number to the left of the decimal (178) as "one hundred seventy-eight."
Follow these words with the word "and."

Step 2

Read the decimal part of the number as "nine." Since there are 3 digits to the right of the decimal, say the word "thousandths" after the word nine.

Step 3

Putting the two parts together, read 178.009 as "one hundred seventy-eight and nine thousandths."

29. B

To determine the mass of the balloon bouquet, you need to add the mass of each balloon and the weight,

$$\begin{pmatrix} 5.75 + 4.15 + 4.756 + 5.25 \\ + 3.893 + 4.58 + 4.184 + 25 \end{pmatrix} = 57.563$$

Therefore, the mass of the entire balloon bouquet, including the mass of the weight, is 57.563 g.

30. A

Step 1

Determine the actual sum, regrouping where necessary.

```
    9 635
    3 099
 +    897
 ─────────
   13 631
```

Step 2

To determine which estimate is closest to the actual sum, find the difference between each estimated sum and the actual sum.

- Emily: 13 631 − 13 500 = 131
- Sarah: 13 631 − 13 000 = 631
- Marcus: 13 631 − 12 500 = 1 131
- Donald: 14 000 − 13 631 = 369

The closest estimate to the actual sum of 13 631 is 13 500 because the difference is only 131. All the other estimates have larger differences: 369, 631, and 1 131.

Emily's estimate is closest to the actual sum.

31. B

Step 1

Identify each number in each set as prime or composite.

A prime number has only two factors: 1 and itself.

A composite number has more than two factors.

- 7 is prime, and 27 is composite.
- 9 is composite, and 19 is prime.
- 3 is prime, and 23 is prime.
- 2 is prime, and 22 is composite.

Step 2

Choose the table that has the numbers correctly classified.

Only the following table has the numbers correctly classified.

Number	9	19
Classification	Composite	Prime

32. D

Step 1

When converting a mixed number to an improper fraction, the first step is to multiply the whole number (13) by the denominator of the fraction (2).

$13 \times 2 = 26$

Step 2

The next step is to add the numerator of the fraction (1) to the product of the whole number and denominator.

$26 + 1 = 27$

Step 3

The number 27 will become the numerator of the improper fraction. The denominator of the improper fraction will be 2 (same as the denominator of the original mixed number).

Expressed as an improper fraction, the mixed number $13\frac{1}{2}$ is $\frac{27}{2}$.

33. A

Calculate the values of the mixed number and the fraction in the first set, $3\frac{3}{4}$ and $\frac{15}{4}$.

Step 1

Calculate the numerator.

Multiply the whole number (3) by the denominator (4), and add the numerator (3) to the product.

$(3 \times 4) + 3 = 15$

Step 2

Write the equivalent improper fraction.

The denominator of the mixed number will be the same denominator for the improper fraction.

$\frac{15}{4}$

The mixed number and the fraction in the set $3\frac{3}{4}$ and $\frac{15}{4}$ have equivalent values.

34. C

Step 1

Determine the ratio of Ashley's candies to the total number of candies.

If Ashley gave 3 candies to Rose, she would then have 12 candies.

$15 - 3 = 12$

Since there are 30 candies in all $(15 + 15 = 30)$, the ratio of Ashley's candies to the total number of candies is 12:30.

Step 2

Reduce the ratio to its lowest terms by dividing both numbers by their greatest common factor (GCF).

In this case, the GCF is 6.

$12 \div 6 = 2$

$30 \div 6 = 5$

The ratio of Ashley's candies to the total number of candies is 2:5.

35. C

Step 1

Identify what is being compared.

The weather on different days is being compared.

Step 2

Determine the order of the terms.

The order is sunny days, then rainy days.

Step 3

Write a ratio.

There were 15 sunny days and 12 rainy days.

The ratio of sunny days to rainy days can be expressed as 15:12.

Step 3

Reduce the ratio to lowest terms.

Divide both terms by their greatest common factor of 3.

$15 \div 3:12 \div 3 = 5:4$

Step 4

Rewrite the ratio using words.

The ratio 5:4 becomes 5 to 4.

The ratio of sunny days to rainy days is 5 to 4.

36. C

Step 1

Determine the length of rope that is cut off.

A percentage is a number out of 100.

Since the length of the rope is 100 m, 25% represents 25 m out of 100 m.

Max cuts off 25 m from the rope that was 100 m long.

Step 2

Determine how much rope is left.

Subtract 25 m from 100 m.

$100 - 25 = 75$

After Max cuts 25% off the rope, 75% of the rope is left, which is 75 m.

The length of the piece of rope that Max has left is 75 m.

37. A

Positive integers are represented to the right of the 0 on a number line. The integers get larger in value as they move away from the 0.
The integers 5 and 8 will be located 5 and 8 units, respectively, to the right of 0.

Negative integers are represented to the left of 0 on a number line. The integers get smaller in value as they move away from the 0.
The integers -12 and -2 will be located 12 and 2 units respectively to the left of the 0.

Number line A shows the correct placement of the given integers.

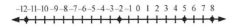

38. A

To determine the descending order of the fractions, convert them into equivalent fractions with a common denominator of 24.

$$\frac{13}{8} = \frac{13 \times 3}{8 \times 3} = \frac{39}{24} \qquad \frac{7}{2} = \frac{7 \times 12}{2 \times 12} = \frac{84}{24}$$

$$\frac{10}{6} = \frac{10 \times 4}{6 \times 4} = \frac{40}{24} \qquad \frac{4}{3} = \frac{4 \times 8}{3 \times 8} = \frac{32}{24}$$

Compare these equivalent fractions according to the values of their numerators.

$$\frac{84}{24}, \frac{40}{24}, \frac{39}{24}, \frac{32}{24}$$

The correct descending order is

$$\frac{7}{2}, \frac{10}{6}, \frac{13}{8}, \frac{4}{3}.$$

39. C

To determine the mass of each doughnut, divide the total mass (655.2) by the number of doughnuts (8).

The mass of each doughnut will be equal to the value of the expression $655.2 \div 8$.

Use long division.

```
      81.9
  8)655.2
     64
     15
      8
     72
     72
      0
```

$655.2 \div 8 = 81.9$

The mass of each individual doughnut is 81.9 g.

40. D

Step 1

Determine the theoretical probability.

Theoretical probability

$$= \frac{\text{favourable outcome}}{\text{total possible outcomes}}$$

Since there are 6 parts in all, there are 6 possible outcomes.

Since there are 2 red parts, there are 2 favourable outcomes.

The theoretical probability is 2 out of 6 or

$$\frac{2}{6} = \frac{1}{3}.$$

Step 2

Determine the experimental probability.

Experimental probability

$$= \frac{\text{number of times an outcome occurs}}{\text{number of times the event was tested}}$$

Since there are 30 spins in all, the number of tests is 30.

Since the spinner stops on red 12 times, the favourable outcome occurs 12 times.

The experimental probability is 12 out of 30 or

$$\frac{12}{30} = \frac{2}{5}.$$

Step 3

Compare the two probability fractions by first making them equivalent fractions.

$$\frac{1}{3} = \frac{5}{15} \text{ and } \frac{2}{5} = \frac{6}{15}$$

The experimental probability is greater than the theoretical probability because $\frac{6}{15} > \frac{5}{15}$.

The experimental probability of the spinner stopping on red is $\frac{1}{15}$ greater than the theoretical probability.

NOTES

Appendices

PART A ANSWER SHEET

This answer sheet has been provided as practice for completing the Year End Part A test. Keep in mind the following instructions:

1. Use an HB pencil to fill the complete circle with dark black markings.
2. In order to change an answer, erase the entire exisiting markings before filling in the new circles.

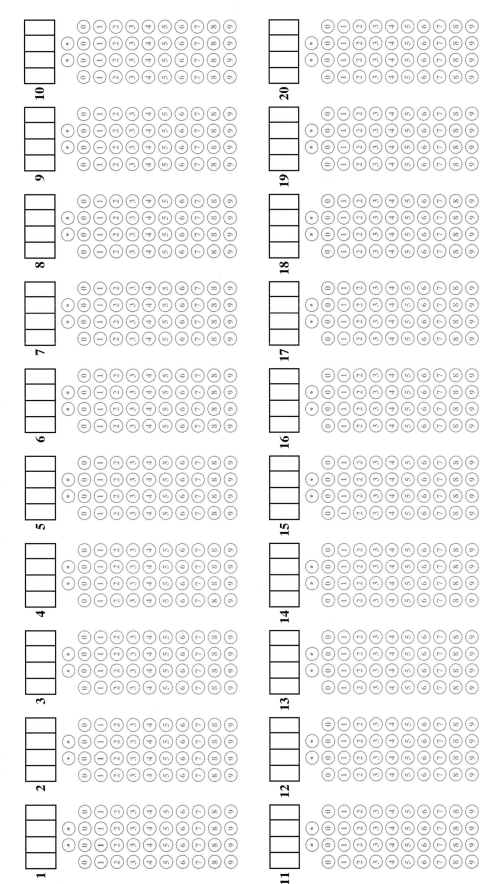

PART A ANSWER SHEET

This answer sheet has been provided as practice for completing the Year End Part A test. Keep in mind the following instructions:
1. Use an HB pencil to fill the complete circle with dark black markings.
2. In order to change an answer, erase the entire existing markings before filling in the new circles.

Cut along line

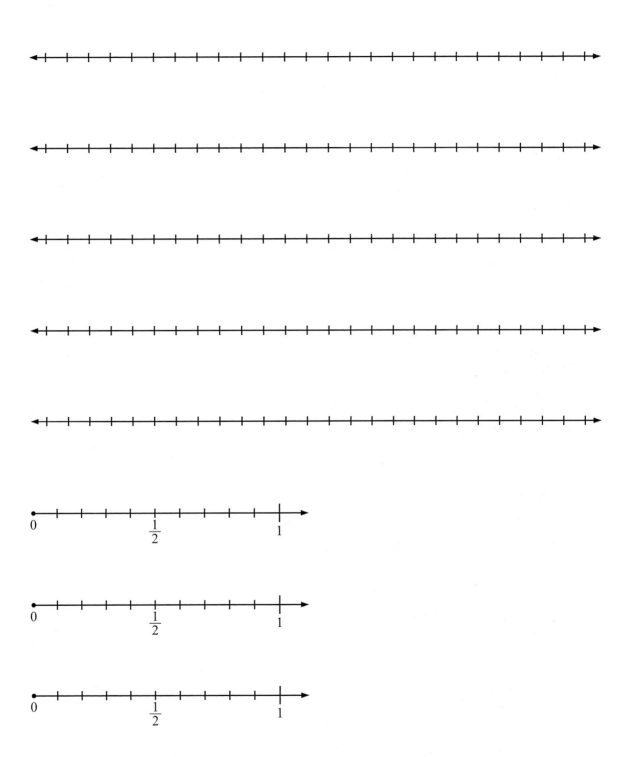

CARTESIAN PLANE – 1ST QUADRANT

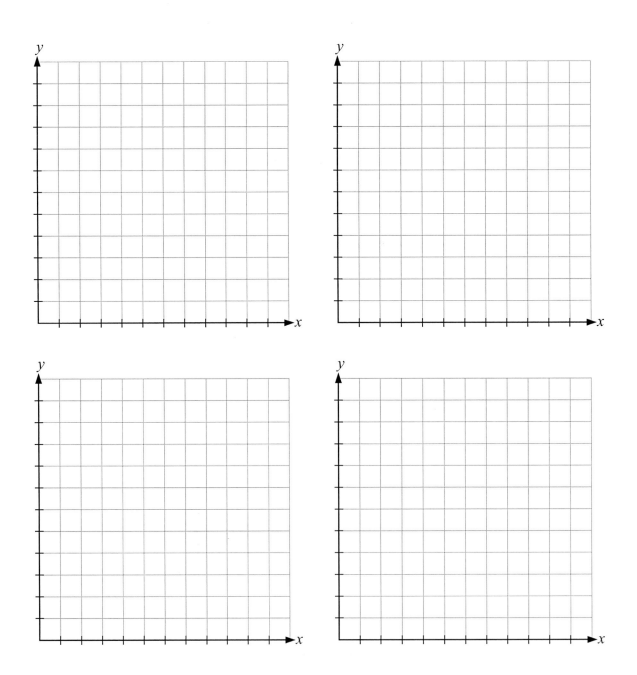

100s Grid

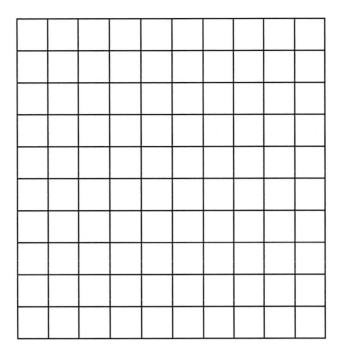

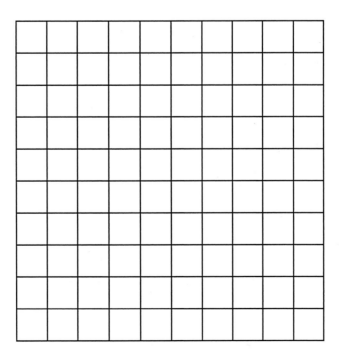

BASE 10 BLOCKS

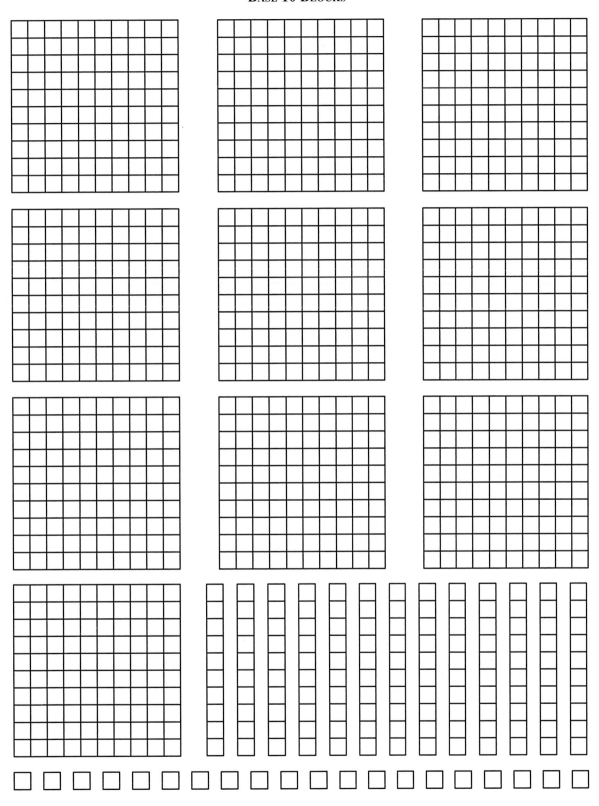

BASE 10 BLOCKS

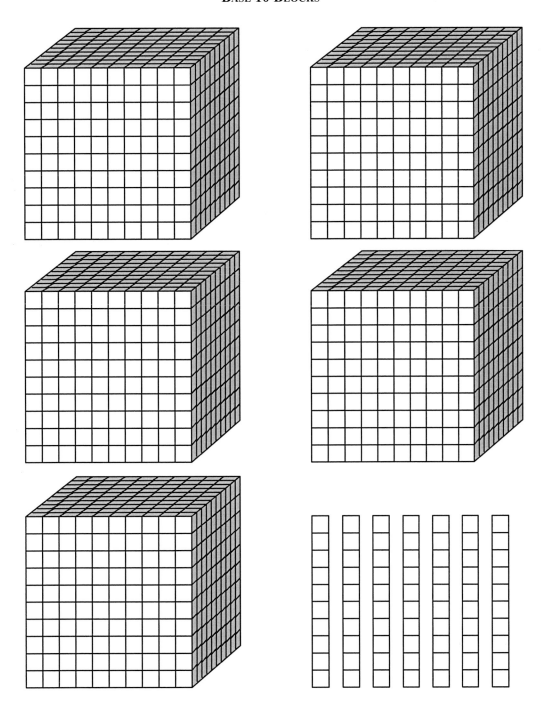

CREDITS

Every effort has been made to provide proper acknowledgement of the original source and to comply with copyright law. However, some attempts to establish original copyright ownership may have been unsuccessful. If copyright ownership can be identified, please notify Castle Rock Research Corp so that appropriate corrective action can be taken.

Some images in this document may be from www.clipart.com, copyright © 2014 Vital Imagery Ltd.

NOTES

NOTES

NOTES

NOTES

NOTES

NOTES

NOTES

BOOK ORDERING INFORMATION
ELEMENTARY and JUNIOR HIGH TITLES

Castle Rock Research offers the following resources to support Alberta students. You can order any of these materials online at:

www.castlerockresearch.com/store

SOLARO - Online Learning		The KEY	SNAP	Prob Solved	Class Notes
$29.95 ea.*		$29.95 ea.*	$29.95 ea.*	$19.95 ea.*	$19.95 ea.*
English Language Arts 9	English Language Arts 6	English Language Arts 9	Science 9	Science 9	Science 9
English Language Arts 8	English Language Arts 5	English Language Arts 6	Mathematics 9	Mathematics 9	Mathematics 9
English Language Arts 7	English Language Arts 4	English Language Arts 3	Mathematics 8	Mathematics 8	Mathematics 8
Mathematics 9	English Language Arts 3	Mathematics 9	Mathematics 7	Mathematics 7	Mathematics 7
Mathematics 8	Mathematics 6	Mathematics 8	Mathematics 6		
Mathematics 7	Mathematics 5	Mathematics 7	Mathematics 5		
Science 9	Mathematics 4	Mathematics 6	Mathematics 4		
Science 8	Mathematics 3	Mathematics 4	Mathematics 3		
Science 7	Science 6	Mathematics 3	*Prices do not include taxes or shipping.*		
Social Studies 9	Science 5	Science 9			
Social Studies 6	Science 4	Science 6			
	Science 3	Social Studies 9			
		Social Studies 6			

Study online using **SOLARO,** with access to multiple courses available by either a monthly or an annual subscription.

The KEY Study Guide is specifically designed to assist students in preparing for unit tests, final exams, and provincial examinations.

The **Student Notes and Problems (SNAP) Workbook** contains complete explanations of curriculum concepts, examples, and exercise questions.

The **Problem Solved** contains exercise questions and complete solutions.

The **Class Notes** contains complete explanations of curriculum concepts.

If you would like to order Castle Rock resources for your school, please visit our school ordering page:

www.castlerockresearch.com/school-orders/